CW00689178

Japan: Described And Illustrated By The Japanese...

Anonymous

Nabu Public Domain Reprints:

You are holding a reproduction of an original work published before 1923 that is in the public domain in the United States of America, and possibly other countries. You may freely copy and distribute this work as no entity (individual or corporate) has a copyright on the body of the work. This book may contain prior copyright references, and library stamps (as most of these works were scanned from library copies). These have been scanned and retained as part of the historical artifact.

This book may have occasional imperfections such as missing or blurred pages, poor pictures, errant marks, etc. that were either part of the original artifact, or were introduced by the scanning process. We believe this work is culturally important, and despite the imperfections, have elected to bring it back into print as part of our continuing commitment to the preservation of printed works worldwide. We appreciate your understanding of the imperfections in the preservation process, and hope you enjoy this valuable book.

JAPAN

JAPAN

DESCRIBED AND ILLUSTRATED BY
THE JAPANESE

*WRITTEN BY EMINENT JAPANESE
AUTHORITIES AND SCHOLARS*

EDITED BY

CAPTAIN F. BRINKLEY

Vol. IV

ILLUSTRATED

J. B. MILLET COMPANY
BOSTON AND TOKYO

Copyright, 1904
By J. B. Millet Company

Entered at Stationers' Hall, London, England

THE NEW YORK
PUBLIC LIBRARY

ASTOR, LENOX AND
TILDEN FOUNDATIONS
R   L

THE UNIVERSITY PRESS, CAMBRIDGE, U. S. A.

CONTENTS

APPENDIX

ILLUSTRATIONS

[vii]

ILLUSTRATIONS

JAPAN

XIX

JAPAN'S COMMERCIAL AND POLITICAL INTERCOURSE WITH FOREIGN COUNTRIES

(Concluded)

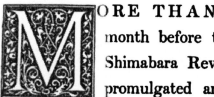ORE THAN A TWELVE-month before the outbreak of the Shimabara Revolt, there had been promulgated an edict of the most drastic nature. It declared that any Japanese subject attempting to go abroad, or any Japanese subject already abroad who attempted to return home, should be executed; it directed that all foreigners professing Christianity should be imprisoned at Omura; it forbade Eurasian children to reside in Japan and it decreed banishment for any persons adopting a Eurasian child and severe punishment for their relatives. Four years later

the Dutch were required to confine themselves
to Deshima. They had succeeded in effectually
prejudicing the Japanese against the Portuguese
and the Spaniards, but they had not succeeded in
preserving any large measure of respect for themselves. These most cruel and illiberal measures
crowned Japan's policy of restriction and isolation — a policy which may be said to have commenced on a radical scale with the proclamation
of Ieyasu in 1614 and to have culminated in the
imprisonment of the Dutch at Deshima in 1641
by his grandson, Iyemitsu, the third Tokugawa
Shogun.

In that interval another step wholly destructive
to maritime enterprise was taken by the same
Iyemitsu. He ordered that all vessels of sea-
going capacity should be destroyed, and that no
craft should thenceforth be built of sufficient size
to venture beyond home waters.

A more complete metamorphosis of a nation's
policy could scarcely be conceived. In 1541 we
find the Japanese celebrated or notorious throughout the whole of the far East for exploits abroad;
we find them known as the "Kings of the Sea;"

[2]

we find them welcoming foreigners with the utmost cordiality and opposing no obstacles whatever to foreign commerce or even to the propagandism of foreign creeds; we find them so quick to recognise the benefits of trade and so apt to pursue them that in the space of a few years they establish commercial relations with no less than twenty over-sea markets; we find them authorising the Portuguese and the English to trade at every port in the empire; we find, in short, all the elements requisite for a career of commercial enterprise, ocean-going adventure and international liberality. In 1641 everything is reversed. Trade is interdicted to all Western people except the Dutch, and they are confined to a little island two hundred yards in length by eighty yards in width. The least symptom of predilection for an alien creed is punished with awful rigour. Any attempt to leave the limits of the realm involves decapitation. Not a ship large enough to pass beyond the shadow of the coast may be built.

For all these changes Christianity was responsible. The policy of seclusion adopted by Japan in the early part of the seventeenth century and resolutely pursued until the middle of the nineteenth was an anti-Christian, not an anti-foreign, policy. The fact cannot be too clearly recognised. It is the chief lesson taught by the events outlined above. Throughout the whole of that period of isolation Occidentals were not known to the Japanese by any of the terms now in common use — as *gwaikoku-jin*, *seiyo-jin* or *i-jin*, which embody the simple meanings, foreigner, Western, alien; they were popularly called *bateren* (padre). Thus completely had foreign intercourse and Christian propagandism become identified in the eyes of the people. And if we remember that "foreign intercourse" associated with Christianity had come to be synonymous in Japanese ears with foreign aggression, the subversal of the Mikado's sacred dynasty and the loss of the independence of the country of the gods, we are in a position to understand the attitude of the nation's mind toward this question.

The commercial story of the Dutch in Deshima need not occupy us long. Their position was practically that of prisoners. An islet of reclaimed land, sixteen thousand yards in area, its

[4]

surface some six feet above high-water mark, constituted their place of residence. The channel separating it from the mainland was spanned by a bridge having a strongly guarded gate at the shoreward end. There the Dutch merchants, numbering from a dozen to a score, were confined under conditions prescribed chiefly with the object of restraining any outward observance of Christianity. Divine services were strictly interdicted as well as every display of religious symbols. No Japanese women, except prostitutes, were permitted to enter this ghetto, nor might any of the Dutch residents leave the islet without due sanction. For the rest, these devotees of commerce experienced sufficiently courteous treatment, and throughout the two centuries of their sojourn they remained absolutely free from the murderous assaults to which foreigners were so frequently subjected after the opening of the country in 1858. It is plain that from the moment when Christianity presented itself to the Japanese in the light of a political agent, an alienator of patriotic sentiment and a perverter of national allegiance, their foreign

[5]

policy was controlled by the necessity of differentiating commerce from religion. They were determined not to trade with any people acknowledging Christian affinities. The English, like the Dutch, were at first exempted from any religious disability, but when, after one failure in the field of Japanese commerce, they attempted to renew the enterprise at a later date (1673), the relationship of their sovereign to the King of Portugal, the home of the Jesuits, proved a fatal objection. The Japanese would have nothing to do with them. It was by the Dutch that this disqualification was urged against the English. Desiring to secure their own monopoly against British competition, they informed the Japanese government that Charles the Second of England was son-in-law to the King of Portugal. The Dutch, in short, contrived with consummate and unscrupulous skill to assist in checking Christian propagandism in Japan and to preserve for themselves alone the privileges of Japanese commerce.

It was, on the whole, a highly profitable though not very extensive privilege. The little community of merchants in Deshima were not

allowed to develop their business without limit.
At no time were the visits of their ships suffered
to exceed two annually, and at the last the
number of vessels was reduced to one a year.
Nevertheless, in the disordered state of Japan's
currency as described above, in the arbitrarily
fixed ratios between gold, silver and copper, and
in the people's ignorance of the value of foreign
manufactures, the Dutch traders found an opportunity which they turned to such good account
that between 1609 and 1858 they are said to
have exported over two hundred million dollars
in gold and silver, as well as two hundred thousand tons of copper. The Japanese of the
present era speak of the Dutch trade as a gate
through which the wealth of the country flowed
away incessantly during a space of nearly two
and a half centuries. Certainly foreign commerce,
under the conditions then existing, never suggested itself as a factor of national prosperity.

Doubtless the reader will not yet have dis-
covered any full explanation of the fact that the
Dutch were so rigidly secluded in the island of
Deshima. Having purged themselves by deed

and declaration from all suspicion of complicity with the Christian propagandists, why should they not have enjoyed the same freedom of trade and residence that was permitted to the Chinese? History, as it has been written for us, does not furnish any conclusive answer to that question, but there is little room to doubt that the considerations which in the nineteenth century dictated the expediency of foreign settlements with narrow limits, were operative in the seventeenth also. The Dutch, following the example of the English, claimed exemption from native criminal jurisdiction, and it was therefore found necessary to segregate them from the Japanese community. Segregation would at any rate have offered the advantages of facilitating the imposition of religious restraints. But that consideration would scarcely have received such strong practical recognition had it not been reënforced by the jurisdictional dilemma. If a society of aliens are to live and trade in a country without being responsible to its penal laws or amenable to its criminal tribunals, it is evidently prudent that they should reside within the im-

[8]

... all suspicion of complicity ... progressives, why should ... enjoyed the same freedom of ... that was permitted to the ... century, as it has been written for us. ... there is any conclusive answer to that ... but there is little room to doubt that ... was which in the nineteenth century ... the excellency of foreign settlements ... powerful, were operative in the seven ... The Dutch, following the example ... desired exemption from native ... jurisdiction, and it was therefore found ... necessary to segregate them from the Japanese ... Segregation would at any rate have ... the advantages of facilitating the impo... ... of revenue restraints. But that consider... ... would scarcely have received such strong ... practical recognition had it not been reinforced ... by the jurisdictional dilemma. If a society ... ... are to live and trade in a country with ... out being responsible to its penal laws or amen... ... able to its criminal tribunals, it is evident ... prudent that they should reside within the li...

SMALL SUMMER HOTEL AT KANAZAWA.

mediate control of their own authorities, and that their contact with the natives should be as restricted as possible. To the exigencies of "extraterritorial jurisdiction," as this peculiar outcome of Occidental and Oriental intercourse is called, the Dutch partly owed their imprisonment in Deshima two and a half centuries ago, and to the same cause European and American merchants, in modern times, wholly owed their imprisonment in the "foreign settlements" of Japan.

One further feature of the Deshima trade must be noted for the sake of the relation it bears to events of our own epoch, namely, the methods of transacting business as dictated by Japanese officials. The popular idea of foreign commerce has already been explained; it was regarded chiefly as the perquisite of a favoured few, not as a factor of national wealth. Evidently the segregation of the foreign agents afforded special facilities for giving effect to that idea. The conduct of the trade could thus be subjected to strict control and its limits rigidly fixed. Without entering into details, which naturally varied from time to time, the Japanese method may be said to have been based on the principle of excluding every element of competition by which the Dutch might profit. The goods imported at Deshima were purchased by a limited number of merchants in Kyoto, Sakai, Osaka, Nagasaki and Yedo, who held special licenses from the government. Skilled appraisers, representing these merchants, visited Nagasaki at the proper season, or resided there permanently. When a cargo arrived it was landed and examined by these appraisers, and their estimates of the market values of the various articles were embodied in a list for submission to the governor of Nagasaki or to delegates of the central government. The list was subsequently handed to the municipal officials, who in turn transmitted it to the Dutch in Deshima, and these on their side indicated their acceptance or rejection of the terms offered. They cannot have employed much latitude of choice in Japan at all events, for they were held in the grip of a virtually inflexible ring; but there remained to them always the alternative of reshipping the goods to some other Eastern market. Thereafter the Japanese agents, acting on behalf of the principals in the towns of which we have spoken, put in tenders for the imports, taking their own original appraisement as an upset figure. Whatever they bid over and above that figure went to the officials. More or less departure from this system is observable at later epochs, but the dominant idea — exclusion of the foreigner from the benefit of Japanese competition — seems to have remained permanently effective.

Insignificant as was the trade at Deshima from a national point of view, and slight as was the traders' contact with the Japanese, it is probable that had that door of ingress been closed to progressive ideas, Japan might not yet have crossed the threshold of her new career. We have seen that the astute founder of the Tokugawa dynasty of *Shoguns* cast the net of his power so deftly over the empire as to entangle all his possible enemies in the meshes of his assured partisans. Successful revolt on the part of an individual feudatory, or successful intrigue by a clique of feudatories, became almost impracticable. He provided effectually against the repetition of that spectacle so familiar to his countrymen, the seizure of administrative authority by one usurper and its speedy transfer to the hands of another amid scenes of turbulence and bloodshed. But the loyal instincts of the people, though lulled to temporary quiescence by the unwonted peace and prosperity resulting from the Tokugawa system, began to reassert themselves in proportion as the horrors of civil war faded into a distant past, and these instincts were constantly reënforced by the suggestions of foreign intercourse and the promptings of national enterprise. On the one hand the people saw the Emperor stripped of all administrative power and relegated to a life of insignificance in Kyoto, while the Tokugawa *Shoguns* exercised autocratic sway in Yedo and enjoyed all the benefits and privileges of authority ; on the other they saw themselves officially excluded from every avenue of maritime and commercial enterprise, while a little band of aliens at Deshima monopolised the foreign trade of the empire, their merchantmen and warships holding the dominion of the seas and their superior scientific knowledge conferring on them advantages too obvious to escape the humblest intelligence. It was inevitable that a spirit of rebellion should grow up against such an artificial and unwholesome state of affairs. The feudal nobles, indeed, did not awake to any perception of the necessity of change. They were either held fast in the vise of Tokugawa authority, or paralysed by the sensuous seductions of the positions they enjoyed and by the machinations of their retainers, who played unceasingly the traditional game of grasping the substance of authority and leaving the shadow only to their lords. It was among these retainers that the longing for a new order of things grew stronger and stronger. Here and there men were found who, at the risk of imprisonment and death, braved the edicts against studying foreign sciences or betraying foreign proclivities, and learned to spell out Dutch books, or diligently gleaned scraps of rare information about the material civilisation of Europe. The story of these courageous and earnest students reads like a romance. At one time we see them puzzling for a week over the import of a Dutch word; at another, laboriously compiling an anatomical vocabulary by fitting terms to the plates in a surgical treatise; now practising rigid economy for months to defray the monstrous cost of some insignificant volume imported by the Hollanders; anon publishing the results of their researches with stealth and apprehension as though to strive after knowledge were criminal. Any one seeking to become acquainted with the quality of Japanese perseverance and moral courage will do well to collect the records of these pioneers of Western civilisation who between 1750 and 1850 gave its first genuine impulse to the great movement of reform in Japan. We are precluded from attempting to trace their history here. Our retrospect must be limited to the general facts that, when an American squadron came, in 1857, to break, by force or by suasion, the barrier of Japanese isolation, the nation was already seething with a spirit of unrest which, though as yet confined to the lower section of the military class, must soon have brought about the changes which the advent of foreigners precipitated.

It has been the habit of Western historians to associate a strong anti-foreign impulse with the movement which culminated in the overthrow of the Tokugawa *Shogunate* and the restoration of administrative authority to the Emperor in 1867. They base that conclusion largely on the fact that the shibboleth of the time was *sonno joi*, which, being interpreted, signifies "reverence the sovereign and expel the stranger." Now, though it is quite true that these two cries were often heard in conjunction, it is by no means true that they were inseparable, or even that the latter had any intimate connection with the former. On the contrary, among the men who constituted the backbone of the agitation for restoring the Imperial administration, there were many who, having acquired, either by actual study or by observation, a full sense of the disadvantages of continued national isolation, aimed not more zealously at the overthrow of the Tokugawa *Shogunate* than at reopening to commercial and maritime enterprise the routes which had been officially closed since the first half of the seventeenth century. We have to understand thus why this liberal element has been hidden from the observation of casual observers, and why the "stranger-expelling" impulse is represented by so many writers as underlying the great revolution of

1867. The explanation is not difficult. Though essentially imperialistic in its prime purpose, the revolution may be called democratic with regard to the *personnel* of those who planned and directed it. They were, for the most part, men without either official rank or social standing. Exponents simply of a theory and being without vicarious aids to push their views, they could not afford to neglect any factor likely to make for the success of their paramount object, the overthrow of the *Shogunate*. Anti-foreign feeling was such a factor. We have analysed the nature of the conviction educated among the Japanese by eighty years of contact with the mediæval methods of Christian propagandism and with the intrigues of foreign commercial rivals. We have seen that the outcome of these experiences was a fierce conviction that the integrity of the empire could be preserved only by keeping out the strangers, the *bateren* (padres), who concealed political treachery under the cloak of religious zeal. Nine out of every ten Japanese *Samurai* held fast by that faith, and would have deemed themselves recusant to the dictates of patriotism had they

[16]

... and difficult. Though
... to its peace purpose, the
... and democratic with regard
... who planned and directed
... for the most part, men without
... . . . social standing. Exponents
... being without vicarious aids
... they could not afford to neg-
... or likely to make for the success of
... paramount object, the overthrow of the
... And foreign feeling was such a fe-
... We have analysed the nature of the convic-
... fostered among the Japanese by eighty years
of contact with the mediaeval methods of Christian
propagandism and with the intrigues of foreign
commercial rivals. We have seen that the outcome of these experiences was a fierce conviction
that the integrity of the empire could be
... only by keeping out the strangers.
... *foreign* (padres), who concealed political
... ery under the cloak of religious zeal. Nine
... of every ten Japanese *Samurai* held fast by
... ... , and would have deemed themselves
... to the dictates of patriotism had they

KIYOMIZU TEMPLE, KYOTO.

failed to exterminate the foreign intruder wherever they found him. The remaining tenth were the little leaven of students and deep thinkers who, looking through the narrow window at Deshima, had caught a glimmering perception of the realities that lay beyond the horizon of their country's prejudice. Now, in the sequence of events, which may be learned from any history, it fell out that the responsibility of violating the traditions of three centuries and throwing down the barriers of national seclusion rested with the Tokugawa government in Yedo. The *Shogun's* ministers signed the treaties with America, England, France and so forth from 1857 onward, and in that act the enemies of the *Shogunate* saw a pretext for winning to their cause all the conservative elements among the *Samurai*. "Let us compass the downfall of the *Shogunate*," they said, "whatever weapons we have to employ for the purpose. The rest will follow in due course." It was thus that the agitation for restoring the Imperial administration came to be ostensibly allied with an anti-foreign movement. If the situation has perplexed subsequent observers, though surveying it with all the wisdom that follows the event, there is not much difficulty in conjecturing how it must have bewildered the foreign diplomatists and statesmen upon whom devolved the duty of dealing with it at the moment. One cannot be surprised that when the torch was set to foreign legations; when foreign subjects and citizens fell under the swords of assassins in broad daylight on public thoroughfares; when vexatious obstacles presented themselves to the enjoyment of privileges promised by treaty, and when official reluctance to be liberal often assumed the semblance of deliberate bad faith, the foreign representatives, with one solitary exception, concluded that the Yedo government was in league with their enemies, and that the whole enigma had its origin in Oriental duplicity. Thus upon the head of the unfortunate administration in Yedo were visited the consequences of crimes perpetrated, in great part, with the unique object of adding to its embarrassments, and foreign governments, by levying fines and imposing humiliations upon the *Shogun*, who was honestly anxious to fulfil his treaty engagements toward them, played unwittingly into the

[18]

hands of those who figured as the foes of foreign intercourse.

Great ends are often promoted by unconscious agents. It was essential for Japan's good that the *Shogunate* should fall, dragging down with it the fabric of military feudalism which must always have presented a powerful obstacle to the spread of progressive ideas and to the unification of the nation. But we may reasonably wish that these changes could have been effected without involving foreigners and Japanese in a labyrinth of mutual misconceptions, and sowing the seeds of prejudices which have borne a wretched crop of antipathy and ill-will. Let it be recorded, however, as a partially redeeming feature, that foreign governments twice. distinguished correctly between friend and foe, and twice struck blows which powerfully contributed to undermine the strength of the anti-foreign sentiment by demonstrating that Japan could not stand for an instant against the warlike resources of Western civilisation. In order to complete this part of our story, we may anticipate the course of events so far as to say that the *Sho-*

gunate fell (1867) almost without a struggle; that feudalism was abolished four years later (1871), the feudal chiefs surrendering their fiefs at the instance of their vassals by whom the revolution had been planned and consummated; that the administration of affairs was resumed by the Emperor with the aid of a cabinet formed of those vassals, and that Japan entered upon a rapid career of liberal progress. Anti-foreign demonstrations ceased as suddenly and completely as though the wand of an omnipotent genius of benevolence had been waved over the land. But anti-foreign feeling did not vanish as quickly as its visible ebullitions. Patriotism is tenacious of existence, and the *Jo-i* sentiment in Japan had its roots in patriotism. We shall see presently that it was afterward perpetuated and even reinspired by causes other than those already noted; but at the time when feudalism fell and the administration was centralised, the leaders of Japanese thought had no purpose closer to their heart than the dissipation of old prejudices and the promotion of international good-will. Some of them had been from the

... without a struggle;
... died four years ...
... its surrendering their ...
... vassals by whom the ...
... pressed and consummated.
... of affairs was resumed by
... the end of a cabinet formed
... that Japan entered upon
... liberal progress. Anti-foreign
... so suddenly and com...
... the wand of an omnipotent
... had been waved over the
... feeling did not vanish as
quickly as ... visible conditions. Patriotism is
... and the *Joi* sentiment is
... patriotism. We sh...
... presently, but ... was afterward perpetua...
and even ... by causes other than the
already noted. ... at the time when feudal...
... and the administration was centralised. ...
... of Japanese thought had no par...
... to their hearts than the dissipation of
... and the promotion of internat...
... Some of them had been from

AN AFTERNOON NAP.

first convinced of the error of isolation; others, starting as vehement disciples of the ancient persuasion, had been converted by the stern lessons of experience, and were fired with all the zeal that marks earnest converts. The method that they adopted to disseminate the tenets of the new liberalism was practical and effective. Wherever among the men of social leading or intellectual light, they saw any one imbued with antipathy to things Occidental, they sent him to travel abroad at the charges of the State. The country's money could not be better spent, they thought, than in educating a disposition essential to the country's welfare. Need it be recorded that these travellers came home as keenly progressive as they had set out obstinately conservative? Often their new convictions proved inconveniently fervent. By way of atonement for their previous mistake they wanted to become pioneers in promoting some special feature of the wonderful civilisation which they had witnessed, and when, as often happened, the State's resources could not bear the strain of so much ardour, or when these too lightly essayed innovations failed of success, there was disappointment merging sometimes into discontent and even scandal. But these things were mere blots upon the broad page of general progress.

From the day when feudalism fell Japan ceased to be an Oriental nation. We do not use the term "Oriental" in a disparaging sense. So far as Japan is concerned, the reader of these pages knows that she possessed a civilisation of her own, — a refined, elaborate and highly developed civilisation, — many phases of which suffer nothing, if indeed they do not gain, by comparison with the civilisation of the foremost Western nations. "Oriental" in this context is employed with reference solely to the conservatism which has come to be regarded as a distinctive feature of East-Asiatic peoples; the conservatism that makes them cling to their old institutions, their old methods, their old laws, their old judicial procedure, their old means of communication, their old social organisation and their old administrative machinery. From the trammels of such conservatism Japan shook herself free in a moment. The soundness of her instincts does not seem to have been impaired by long exile from international competition and long lack of invigorating contact with foreign intellects. She knew the good when she saw it, and she chose it unhesitatingly without racial prejudice or false shame. It is possible, of course, to set forth an imposing catalogue of achievements verifying these assertions — a catalogue of laws compiled, judicial tribunals organised, parliamentary institutions introduced, railways built, telegraphs erected, postal services established, industrial enterprises developed, lines of steamers opened, educational systems started, a newspaper press created, and so forth. We shall have occasion presently to make special allusion to some of these things, but it is not with statistics that we wish to deal here so much as with the broad fact that Japan has differentiated herself completely from "Oriental nations," in the usually accepted sense of the term, and that her aspirations, her modes of thought, her impulses, her ideals and her tests of conduct must now be classed — not altogether, indeed,

[23]

but certainly in the main—as Occidental. She may be regarded as a Western nation situated on the confines of the far East,—a nation now, for the second time in its history, giving free play to the instincts of progress, of enterprise and of daring which, conspicuously displayed three centuries ago, were thereafter paralysed by causes for which the Christian Occident, not the "pagan" Orient, is primarily responsible.

AMMA—SAN, OR BLIND SHAMPOOER.

JAPAN

... certainly is the ... —... to all ... ...
... be regarded as a Western nation stand ...
... ... of the Far East.—... then now,
... the second time in its history, giving free
... to the instincts of progress, of enterprise
... of daring which, conspicuously displayed
... centuries ago, were thereafter paralysed by
... ... for which the Christian Occident of the
... ... is primarily responsible.

AMMA—SAN, OR BLIND SHAMPOOER.

XX

THE ATTITUDE OF JAPAN TOWARD FOREIGN RESIDENTS—JAPANESE FINANCE

THE REOPENING OF JAPAN to intercourse with the outer world was attended by a difficulty for which readers of what has been written above on the subject of currency will not be unprepared. In order to conduct tradal operations in this long-secluded country some arrangement had to be made as to tokens of exchange. Practically the system pursued by the Dutch had been based simply on the weight of precious metal contained in Japanese coins, independently of their denominations and without any attempt to secure the circulation of foreign monetary tokens. The same system, so far as concerned weight, was adopted in 1858, but was supplemented by a provision that foreign coins should have currency in Japan. Foreign coins, the treaty said, must pass current for corresponding weights in Japanese coin of the same description, — gold for gold, silver for silver, — and during a period of one year after the opening of the ports the Japanese government must furnish to foreigners Japanese coins in exchange for theirs, equal weights being given and no discount taken for recoinage. This arrangement altogether ignored the ratio between the precious metals in the Japanese coinage system, and as the ratio stood at five to one, whereas the ratio then ruling in Europe was fifteen to one, it resulted that the foreigner acquired the right of purchasing gold with silver in Japan at one third of the former's price in the Occident. To state the facts more explicitly, the treaty enabled foreigners to buy with one hundred and twenty-five dollar-cents' worth of silver four Japanese silver tokens (called *bu*) which, in the Japanese coinage system, were exchangeable for a gold coin (called *koban*) intrinsically worth three times as much. Of course the treaty could not have been framed with the deliberate intention of securing to foreigners such an unjust advan-

[26]

tage. As a result of long isolation, Japan's stores of the precious metals were not connected by the relation governing their interchangeable values in Europe, and foreign statesmen, when negotiating commercial treaties with her, cannot have had any idea of holding her to that particular outcome of her inexperience. Indeed, the treaty did not create any explicit right of the kind, for although it provided that foreign coins should be exchangeable against Japanese, weight for weight, it contained no provision as to the denominations of Japanese coins or the ratio of the precious metals in the Japanese monetary system.

The Japanese government, seeing the country threatened with the speedy exodus of all its gold, adopted an obvious remedy. It issued a new silver coin bearing the same denomination as the old but weighing three times as much. In short, it exercised a right which every independent nation would claim, the right of so modifying its currency, when suddenly brought into circulation with foreign coins, as to preserve a due ratio between gold and silver, and thus prevent the former's being drained out of the country at one third of its intrinsic value. Nevertheless this equitable view of the case did not·commend itself to the men who looked to profit by the old conditions. They raised a vehement protest against what they called "a gross violation of treaty rights" and "a deliberate attempt on the part of the Japanese authorities to raise the price of all native produce two hundred per cent against the foreign purchaser." There is documentary evidence that the foreign representatives appreciated the difficulties of Japan's position. None the less they held her to the unfair version of her agreement. She had to revert to coins of the old standard, and though she bowed to the necessity, the result of this complication was an abiding sense of injustice on her side, and an impression on that of the foreign resident that she had dishonestly sought to evade her engagements. Nothing, indeed, is more striking than the distrust that pervaded the whole attitude of the foreigner toward the Japanese in those early days. The worst construction was put upon their acts, whether official or private, and even when recording the

BOYS PLAYING HOCKEY.

BOYS PLAYING KOTORO.

adoption of some liberal course by the Tokyo government, the foreign representatives generally qualified their approval by a hope that no trickery or abuse was intended. It is plain that they had strong reasons for their want of confidence. The Tokugawa Regent, while faithfully willing to implement his treaty promises, was compelled by the exigencies of domestic policy to simulate an attitude of unwillingness.

The advocates of overthrowing feudalism and restoring the Emperor's administrative authority endeavoured constantly to embroil the regency with foreign powers by throwing obstacles in the path of smooth intercourse and by acts of violence against individual foreigners. The people, too subservient to take any initiative of their own, too shrewd to turn their backs wholly on the profits of commerce, seemed at one time to be playing into the hands of anti-foreign officials, at another to be implicitly following the instincts of sound business. In the absence of any accessible gauge of public opinion, foreign observers had to rely upon rumour and conjecture, and every estimate of the situation was naturally coloured by a suspicion that three centuries of anti-foreign prejudice could not have been replaced, at a moment's notice, by a genuine desire for free intercourse. Still, when the fullest allowance is made for all these factors of friction, it is not to be denied that the behaviour of foreigners themselves was scarcely calculated to conciliate the Japanese.[1] Time, of course, corrected many

[1] A more trustworthy witness on this subject cannot be cited than Sir Rutherford Alcock, the first British representative in Japan. Writing to the British foreign secretary at the close of 1859, he said : " Looking, indeed, to the indiscreet conduct, to use the mildest term, of many if not all the foreign residents, the innumerable and almost daily recurring causes of dispute and irritation between the Japanese officials of all grades and the foreign traders, both as to the nature of the trade they enter into and the mode in which they conduct it, open in many instances to grave objection, I cannot wonder at the existence of much ill-feeling. And when to those sources of irritation and animosity among the official classes are added the irregularities, the violence and the disorders, with the continual scenes of drunkenness, incidental to seaports where sailors from men-of-war and merchant ships are allowed to come on shore, sometimes in large numbers, I confess, so far from sharing in any sweeping conclusions to the prejudice of the Japanese, I think the rarity of such retaliative acts of violence on their part is a striking testimony in their favour. . . . Our own people and the foreigners generally take care that there shall be no lack of grounds of distrust and irritation. Utterly reckless of the future ; intent only on profiting if possible by the present moment to the utmost ; regardless of treaties or future consequences, they are wholly engaged just now in shipping off all the gold currency of Japan. . . . Any coöperation, therefore, with the diplomatic agents of their respective countries in their efforts to lay the foundations of permanent, prosperous and mutually beneficial commerce between Japan and Western nations is out of the question. On the contrary, it is the merchants who, no doubt, create the most serious difficulties. It may be all very natural and what was to have been anticipated, but it is not the less embarrassing. And in estimating the difficulties to be overcome in

of the evil influences operative in early days, but there is neither sense nor justice in claiming, as has been so often claimed by modern writers, that the foreigner residing in Japan has always been sinned against and never sinning in his dealings and doings. He has undoubtedly conferred on Japan an immense benefit by building up for her a trade which, without his experience, energy and capital, must have remained comparatively insignificant. But, on the other hand, his method has been masterful; his mood suspicious; his judgment harsh and unsympathetic; his scale of living so far above that of the Japanese merchant as to suggest an exaggerated estimate of the profit derived by him from their mutual commerce; and his persistent use of Chinese employees in positions of trust, to the exclusion of Japanese, has suggested a contemptuous and distrustful estimate of native capacities and integrity. There has thus been a steady

any attempt to improve the aspect of affairs, if the ill-disguised enmity of the governing classes and the indisposition of the executive government to give practical effect to the treaties be classed among the first and principal of these, the unscrupulous character and dealings of foreigners who frequent the ports for the purposes of trade are only second and, from the sinister character of the influence they exercise, scarcely inferior in importance."

effort on the Japanese side to eliminate the foreign middleman and transfer to native hands the share now taken by him in the country's over-sea trade. That point will presently be illustrated by figures; but we pass on now to trace the outlines of a question which, though in one sense independent of trade and tradal relations, seems to fall naturally into the context of this part of our subject.

It has always been considered expedient, and certainly it is wise, that the subjects and citizens of Occidental Christian states, when visiting or inhabiting Oriental countries which are not Christian, should be exempted from the penalties and procedure prescribed by the latter's criminal law; should, in short, continue to enjoy, even within the territories of such countries, the privilege of being arraigned before tribunals of their own nationality and tried by judges of their own race. In pursuance of that principle the various powers having treaties with Oriental nations establish Consular Courts within the latter's borders, and the jurisdiction exercised by these courts is called "extra-territorial" to

FLOODING AN IRIS GARDEN (NEAR TOKYO) BY MAN POWER.

distinguish it from the jurisdiction exercised by native, or territorial, tribunals. The system was applied to Japan's case, as a matter of course, in 1858. One of its results was that the foreign residents had to be confined in settlements grouped about their Consular Courts, for it would have been plainly imprudent that they should be granted free access to provincial districts distant by perhaps scores or even hundreds of miles from the only tribunals competent to control them. The Japanese raised no objection at the outset to this system. They recognised that neither the character of their laws nor the methods of their law courts warranted any alternative. But, as a patriotic, self-respecting nation, they determined that no effort should be spared to qualify for the exercise of a right which is among the fundamental attributes of every sovereign state, the right of judicial autonomy. Under any circumstances the recasting of their laws and the reorganisation of their law courts would have occupied a prominent place in the programme of general reform suggested by contact with the Western world, but the "extra-territorial" question certainly stirred them to special legislative efforts, for, apart from the irksomeness of consular jurisdiction as a badge of inferior civilisation on the part of the country where it is exercised, numerous abuses and anomalies are incidental to the system itself. Without entering into these particulars, it will suffice to say here that, after much labour and research, the Japanese elaborated excellent codes of criminal and civil law, excerpting the best features of European jurisprudence and adapting them to the conditions and usages of the country; and that they remodelled their law courts, taking steps also to educate a judiciary whose members, though falling appreciably short of Anglo-Saxon standards, were not incompetent to discharge the duties devolving on them. Then Japan asked for the abolition of consular jurisdiction; asked that all within her borders, without distinction of nationality, should be subject to her laws and judicable by her law courts, as all persons, of whatever nationality, found within the borders of every sovereign state in the West are subject to its laws and judicable by its law courts; and she supplemented her application by a promise that its favourable reception should be the signal for the complete opening of the country and the removal of all restrictions hitherto imposed on foreign trade, travel and residence in her realm. She said, in brief, to Western powers, "Recognise the efforts I have made to be worthy of your trust, and I, on my side, will entirely abandon the isolation which you yourselves have always condemned so vehemently as inconsistent with civilised principles." That was turning the tables very effectually.

From the first it had been the habit of Occidental peoples to upbraid Japan on account of the barriers opposed by her to foreign intercourse, and she was now able to claim that the barriers were no longer created by her intention or maintained by her desire, but that they existed because of a system which theoretically proclaimed her unfitness for free association with Western nations, and practically made it impossible for her to throw open her territories completely for the ingress of strangers. A portly volume might be filled with the details of the negotiations that followed Japan's proposal. Never before had an Oriental State sought such recognition, and there was the utmost reluctance on the part of Western powers to try the unprecedented experiment of intrusting the lives and property of their subjects and citizens to the keeping of a "pagan" people. Even the outlines of the story cannot be sketched here, though it abounds with diplomatic curiosities and though several of its incidents do as much credit to Japan's patience and tact as its *finale* does to the justice and liberality of Occidental governments. There is, however, one page of the history that calls for brief notice since it supplies a key to much which would otherwise be inexplicable. The respect entertained by a nation for its own laws and the confidence it reposes in their administrators are in direct proportion to the efforts it has expended upon the development of the former and the education of the latter. Foreigners residing in Japan naturally clung to "extra-territorial" jurisdiction as a privilege of inestimable value. They saw, indeed, that such a system could not be

permanently imposed on a country where the
conditions justifying it had nominally disappeared,
but they saw, also, that the legal and judicial
reforms effected by Japan had been crowded into
an extraordinarily brief period, and that, as tyros
experimenting with alien systems, the Japanese
might be betrayed into many errors. A struggle
thus ensued between foreign distrust on the one
side and Japanese aspirations on the other — a
struggle often developing painful phases. For
whereas the case for the foreign resident stood
solid and rational so long as it rested on the
basis of his proper attachment to the laws and
the judiciary which the efforts of his nationals
through long generations had rendered worthy
of trust and reverence, and on the equally intelligible and reasonable ground that he wanted con-
vincing proofs of Japan's competence to discharge
her novel functions with discretion and impartiality
before submitting to her jurisdiction, it ceased to
be a solid and rational case when its champions
undertook not merely to exaggerate the risks of
trusting Japan implicitly, but also to prove her
radical unworthiness of any trust whatever and

[37]

to depict her under aspects so deterrent that to pass under her jurisdiction assumed the character of a catastrophe.

The struggle lasted fourteen years, but its gist is contained in this brief statement. The foreign resident, whose affection for his own systems was measured by the struggle their evolution had cost, and whose practical instincts forbade him to take anything on trust where security of person and possession was concerned, would have stood out a wholesomely conservative and justly cautious figure had not his attitude been disfigured by local journalists who in order to justify his conservatism allowed themselves to be betrayed into the constant *rôle* of blackening Japan's character and suggesting harshly prejudiced interpretations of her acts and motives. It is one thing to hesitate before entering a new house until its habitable qualifications have been ascertained. It is another thing to condemn it without trial as radically and necessarily deficient in such qualifications. The latter was, in effect, the line often taken by the noisiest opponents of Japan's claims, and of course no little resentment and indignation were aroused on the side of the Japanese, who, chafing against the obvious antipathies of their foreign critics and growing constantly more impatient of the humiliation to which their country was internationally condemned, were sometimes prompted to displays of resentment which became new weapons in the hands of their critics. Throughout this struggle the government and citizens of the United States always showed conspicuous sympathy with Japanese aspirations, and it should also be recorded that, with exceptions so rare as to establish the rule, foreign tourists and publicists discussed the problem liberally and fairly, perhaps because, unlike the foreign communities resident in Japan, they had no direct interest in its solution. At last,[1] after long years

[1] It would be incorrect to suppose that the responsibility for the delay can be thrown entirely on the foreign side. More than once an agreement reached the verge of conclusion, when Japanese public opinion, partly incited by political intrigues, rebelled vehemently against the guarantees demanded of Japan, and the negotiations were interrupted in consequence, not to be again resumed until a considerable interval had elapsed. This point will easily be understood when we say that whereas, at the outset of the discussion, Japanese officialdom had the matter entirely in its own hands and might have settled it on any basis, however liberal to foreigners, without provoking, for the moment at all events, seriously hostile criticism on the part of the nation, there gradually grew up among the people *pari passu* with journalistic development, with the study of international law and with the organisation of political parties, a

of diplomatic negotiation and public discussion,
European governments conceded the justice of
Japan's demands, and it was agreed that from
July, 1899, subject to the previous fulfilment of
certain conditions,[1] Japanese tribunals should assume jurisdiction over every person of whatever
nationality within the confines of Japan and the
whole country should be thrown open to foreigners,
the " Settlements " being abolished and all limita-
tions upon trade, travel and residence removed
throughout the length and breadth of the realm.
The sequel of the story is still in the lap of the
future at the time of writing this record. It
would be rash to forecast the result of an unprecedented experiment. There is one comment to
be made, however. It is that the mood of many

strong sense of what an independent state has a right to expect, and
thus the longer the negotiations were protracted the keener became the
popular scrutiny to which they were subjected and the greater the
general reluctance to indorse any irksome concessions. Had foreign
diplomacy recognised the growth of that sentiment and been content to
take moderate advantage of the Japanese negotiators' mood, the issue
might have been comparatively satisfactory to foreigners. But by asking
too much and haggling too long, Western statesmen lost their opportunity
of obtaining any substantial guarantees, and had ultimately to hand over
their nationals to Japanese jurisdiction on pure trust.

[1] The main, indeed the only notable, condition was that the whole of
the new Japanese codes of law must have been in operation for a period
of at least one year before the abolition of consular jurisdiction.

... to foreigners,
... all limita-
... are removed
... of the realm.
... in the hp of the
... moved. It
... result of an unpre-
... is one comment to
... that the ... of many

... has ... to resort, and
... deserted the scenes because the
... ... and the greater the
... foreign
... growth of the ... en content to
... on the Jacent ... ego ... ed, the base
... their foreigners. But by ... ing
... Weak ... under their opportunity
... realm ... hand over
... ...

... the whole of
... of his must have ... in op ... for a period
... fore the abolition of ... jurisdiction

[81]

KAGO BEARERS.

members of the foreign communities toward the new system greatly diminishes the chances of its smooth working. Where a captious and aggrieved disposition exists, opportunities to find fault and discover causes of complaint will not be wanting. The demeanour of the Japanese, also, on the eve of this great change is not altogether reassuring. Among the student and labouring classes a recrudescence of anti-foreign feeling has made itself apparent, not in the sense of the old "alien-expelling" tradition, but rather in the nature of an impulse of self-assertion which, though not unnatural under the circumstances, too often assumes a rude and truculent character not calculated to conciliate the foreign resident or to dispel his misgivings.

These diplomatic questions and the controversies that grew out of them did not interfere with the development of the country's foreign trade. In that field a fair prospect presented itself from the outset. Japan produces silk of specially fine quality, and it happened that, just before her supplies of that staple became available for export, the production of the

"noble article" in France and Italy had been
largely curtailed owing to a new disease of the
silkworm. Thus, when the first bales of Japanese
silk appeared in London and it was found to
possess qualities superior not only to the silk of
Bengal and China but even to anything hitherto
known in Europe, a keen demand sprung up for
it, and as early as 1863 — the fourth year after the
inauguration of the trade — no less than twenty-
six thousand bales were sent out of the country.
Japanese tea also found a market abroad, chiefly
in the United States, and six million pounds
were shipped in 1863. The corresponding figures
for these two staples in 1897 were sixty-nine
thousand bales and twenty-seven million pounds,
respectively. That remarkable development
is typical of the general history of Japan's foreign
trade. Omitting the first decade, during which
various abnormal factors were of course operative, we find that the volume of the trade grew
from twenty-six million *yen* in 1868 to three hundred and eighty-two millions in 1897. It was
not by any means a uniform growth, however.
On the contrary, the period of thirty years

(1868–97) divides itself conspicuously into two eras: the first of eighteen years (1868–85) during which the growth was from twenty-six to sixty-six millions, a ratio of one to two and one half, approximately; the second of twelve years (1885–97) during which the growth was from sixty-six to three hundred and eighty-two millions, a ratio of nearly one to six. What was the chief cause of such unequal expansion? Why should a commerce which only doubled itself in eighteen years have sextupled itself in the next twelve? That is a question the answer to which possesses interest, not merely in this context, but also for independent reasons.

When the administrative power reverted to the Emperor in 1867, the central treasury was absolutely empty. It is not to be supposed that the funds hitherto employed for governmental purposes in the fiefs began at once to flow into the coffers of the State. On the contrary, the feudal nobles retained their principalities; the *Shogun* his domains; the temples their estates. The revenues accruing from these various sources continued to be collected and employed as before without any reference to the needs of the new Imperial administration. The agricultural classes were then paying taxes that aggregated two hundred and twenty million *yen* annually, — according to present rates and prices, — and merchants and manufacturers were subject to levies of greater or less magnitude as official necessity arose. In short, the taxable resources of the nation were pretty fully exploited for the support of the feudal system. The *Shogun*, who represented the apex of the system, abdicated, but did not hand over to the sovereign, his administrative successor, either the contents of his treasury or the control of the lands from which he derived his income. He contended, not without reason, that funds for the government of the nation as a whole should be levied from the people at large. Partly owing to this complication, and partly owing to the obstinacy of some of the *Shogun's* stanchest vassals, swords were drawn, and the impecunious ministry of the Emperor had to organise a campaign which, though followed by confiscations placing the government in command of certain limited sources of revenue, had also the effect of increasing its immediate embarrassments. No exit from the dilemma offered except an issue of paper money. This was not a novelty in Japan. Paper money had been known to the people since the middle of the seventeenth century, and in the era of which we are now writing no less than sixteen hundred and ninety-four varieties of notes were circulated in the two hundred and seventy-seven fiefs. There were gold notes, silver notes, *cash*-notes, rice-notes, umbrella-notes, ribbon-notes, lathe-article-notes, and so on through an interminable list, the circulation of each kind being limited to the confines of the issuing fief. Many of these notes had almost ceased to have any purchasing power, and nearly all were regarded by the people as evidences of official greed and unscrupulousness. The first duty of a centralised, progressive administration should have been to reform the currency; to substitute uniform and sound media of exchange for these multitudinous and unsecured tokens, which hampered trade, destroyed credit and opposed barriers to commercial intercourse between neighbouring provinces and districts. The political leaders of the time appreciated that duty, but instead of proceeding to discharge it, saw themselves compelled by stress of circumstances to adopt the very device which, in the hands of the feudal chiefs, had involved such deplorable results. It was an irksome necessity, and the new government sought to relieve its conscience and preserve its moral prestige by pretending that the object of the issue was to encourage wealth-earning enterprise, and that the notes would be lent to the fiefs for the purpose of promoting commerce and industry. The people appraised these euphemisms at their true worth, and the new notes fell to a discount of fifty per cent. Then ensued a brief but sharp struggle between rulers and ruled. The government resorted to arbitrary measures, sometimes of great severity, to force its notes into circulation at par with silver. But there was no continuity of policy. One day men were imprisoned for discounting paper tokens; the next they were released. In December, the authorities officially recognised a depreciation of twenty per cent; in the following April they withdrew the recognition and proclaimed the equality of specie and paper. Now they promised to redeem the notes in thirteen years; then they shortened the period to five, and again they postponed it indefinitely. Nothing is more astonishing than the fact that, despite this bewilderment and vacillation, the government's financial credit gradually acquired strength, so that within five years, though the issues of paper money aggregated nearly sixty million *yen*, it circulated freely throughout the whole empire at par with silver, and even commanded at one time a small premium.

It is true that by this epoch the revenues of all the fiefs had become available for the service of the State, and that only one tenth of their total had been appropriated for the support of the territorial nobles, now deprived of all administrative functions and reduced to the rank of private gentlemen, without either titles to distinguish them from their former vassals or estates to give them local prestige. But the central government, having reduced taxation to about one fourth of its former total, found the public income too small for the expenditures. The paper money of the fiefs, amounting to twenty-five million *yen*, had been exchanged for treasury notes. The building of railways had been commenced. The foundations of an army and a navy had been laid. A postal system, a telegraph system, a prison system, a police system and an educational system had been organised. The construction of roads, the improvement of harbours, the lighting and buoying of the coast had been vigorously undertaken. A mercantile marine had been created. Public works had been inaugurated on a considerable scale. Many industrial enterprises had been started under official auspices as object lessons to the people, and large sums in aid of similar projects had been lent to private persons. The government, living far beyond its income, had unavoidable recourse to further issues of fiduciary paper, and in proportion as the volume of the latter exceeded the actual currency requirements of the time, its value depreciated until in 1881, fourteen years after the Restora-

REST—HOUSE ON NOGE HILL, ABOVE YOKOHAMA, IN CHERRY—BLOSSOM TIME.

tion, notes to the face value of one hundred and thirty-five million *yen* had been put into circulation; the treasury possessed specie of only eight and one half millions, and eighteen paper *yen* could be purchased with ten silver coins of the same denomination. Up to that year fitful efforts had been made to strengthen the specie value of fiat paper by throwing quantities of gold and silver upon the market from time to time, and large sums — totalling twenty-three million *yen* — had been devoted to the promotion of industries whose products, it was hoped, would go to swell the lists of exports and thus draw metallic money to the country.

But these superficial devices were now finally abandoned, and the government applied itself steadfastly to reducing the volume of the fiduciary currency, on the one hand, and accumulating a specie reserve, on the other. The steps of the programme were simple. By applying the pruning knife boldly to administrative expenditures; by transferring certain charges from the treasury to the local communes; by suspending all grants in aid of provincial public

works and private enterprises, and by a moderate
increase of the tax on alcohol, an annual surplus of revenue totalling seven and one half
million *yen* was secured. This was applied to
reducing the volume of the notes in circulation.
At the same time it was resolved that all
officially conducted industrial and agricultural
works should be sold — since their purpose of
instruction and example seemed now to have
been sufficiently achieved — and the proceeds,
together with various securities (aggregating
twenty-six million *yen* in face value) held by
the treasury, should be applied to the purchase
of specie. The latter was a delicate and difficult operation. Had the government entered
the market openly as a seller of its own fiduciary notes, its credit must have suffered. There
were, also, ample reasons to doubt whether any
available stores of precious metal remained in
the country. In obedience to elementary economical laws, the cheap money had steadily
driven out the dear, and although the government mint at Osaka, founded in 1871, had
struck eighty million *yen* of gold and silver

coins between that date and 1881, when the policy of which we are now speaking was inaugurated, the customs returns showed that the whole of this metallic currency had flowed out of the country. Under these circumstances Japanese financiers decided that only one course offered. The treasury must play the part of national banker. Products and manufactures destined for export must be purchased by the State with fiduciary notes, and the metallic proceeds of their sales abroad must be collected and stored in the treasury. The outcome of these various arrangements was that, by the middle of 1885, the volume of fiduciary notes had been reduced to one hundred and nineteen million *yen*, their depreciation had fallen to three per cent, and the metallic reserve of the treasury had increased to forty-five million *yen*. The resumption of specie payments was then announced, and became, in the autumn of that year, an accomplished fact.

XXI

THE ATTITUDE OF JAPAN TOWARD FOREIGN RESIDENTS — JAPANESE FINANCE

(*Concluded*)

E HAVE DWELT UPON THIS chapter of Japan's modern history at some length, not merely because it sets forth a fine feat of finance, indicating clear insight, good organising capacity and courageous energy, but also because volumes of adverse foreign criticism were written into its margin during the course of the incidents it embodies. A score of onlooking strangers were prepared each with an infallible nostrum of his own, the rejection of which convinced him of Japan's hopeless stupidity. Now she was charged with robbing her own people because she bought their goods with paper money and sold them for specie; again she was accused of an official conspiracy to ruin the foreign local banks because

XXI

... OF JAPAN TOWARD FOREIGN
... JAPANESE FINANCE
(Concluded)

... HAVE DWELT UPON THIS

... of Japan's modern history
... ... length, not merely because
... ... forth a true test of financa
... ... good organising capacity
... ... but also because volumes
of adverse ... criticism were written into its
... during the course of the incidents it em-
bodies. A score of onlooking strangers were
prepared each with an infallible nostrum of his
own, the rejection of which convinced him of
Japan's hopeless stupidity. Now she was charged
... robbing her own people because she bought
their goods with paper money and sold them in
specie; again she was accused of an official con-
spiracy to ruin the foreign local banks because

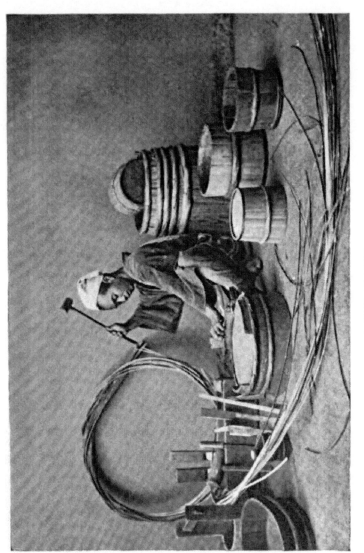

A TUB MAKER.

she purchased exporters' bills on Europe and America at rates that defied ordinary competition; and while some declared that she was plainly without any understanding of her own doings, others predicted that she could not possibly extricate herself from the slough of an inflated and largely depreciated fiat currency without recourse to European capital, and agreed that her heroic method of dealing with the problem would paralyse industry, interrupt trade, produce widespread suffering, and, in short, bring about the advent of the proverbial seven devils. Undoubtedly, to carry the currency of a nation from a discount of seventy or eighty per cent to par in the course of four years, reducing its volume at the same time from one hundred and thirty-five to one hundred and nineteen millions, was a financial enterprise violent and daring almost to rashness. The gentler expedient of a foreign loan — an expedient of recently proved efficacy in Italy's case — would have commended itself to the majority of economists. But it may be here stated, once for all, that until her adoption of gold monometallism in 1897, the foreign money market was practically closed to Japan. Had she borrowed abroad, it must have been on a sterling basis. Receiving a fixed sum in silver, she would have had to discharge her debt in rapidly appreciating gold. Twice, indeed, she had recourse to London for small sums, but when she came to cast up her accounts, the cost of the accommodation stood out in deterrent proportions.[1] These considerations were supplemented by a strong aversion to incurring pecuniary obligations to Western States before the latter consented to restore her judicial and tariff autonomy. The example of Egypt showed what kind of fate might overtake a semi-independent State falling into the clutches of foreign bondholders. Japan did not wish to fetter herself with foreign debts while struggling to emerge from the ranks of Oriental powers. After all, nothing succeeds like success. Japanese financiers made a signal success. Having undertaken to reorganise the administration of an

---

[1] A nine-per-cent loan placed on the London market in 1868 and paid off by 1882 produced 4,782,400 yen, and cost, altogether, 11,869,513 yen; and a seven-per-cent loan issued in 1872 and paid off in 1897 produced 10,832,400 yen, and cost, altogether, 36,000,000 yen, approximately.

empire and inaugurate a vast programme of reform, they met the difficulty of an empty treasury by issuing fiat notes, and then, fourteen years later, grappling boldly with the problem of this inflated and heavily depreciated currency, they restored its value to par and resumed specie payments in the brief space of four years. This brings us back to the point at which we digressed to speak of the currency question.

The volume of the foreign trade grew from twenty-six million *yen* in 1868 to forty-nine millions in 1875, and developed so slowly during the next decade that, after vibrating between the latter figure and sixty-seven millions, it became almost stationary, so that the public began to despair of any large growth, and the fair prospects of the early days faded out of sight. Yet there was good reason to wonder that trade could continue at all under the circumstances. Against the import merchant the currency trouble worked with double potency. Not only did the gold with which he purchased goods appreciate constantly in terms of the silver for which he sold them, but the silver itself appreciated sharply and rapidly in terms of the fiat notes paid by Japanese consumers. Cursory reflection may suggest that these factors should have operated inversely to stimulate exports as much as they depressed imports. But such was not altogether the case in practice. For the exporters' transactions were always hampered by the possibility that a delay of a week or even a day might increase the purchasing power of his silver by bringing about a further depreciation of paper, and it was not till this element of pernicious disturbance was removed that the trade recovered a healthy tone and grew so lustily that in 1897 its volume aggregated three hundred and eighty-two million *yen*, thus treading close on the heels of the foreign commerce of China, with her three hundred million inhabitants and long-established international relations.

Two questions of prime interest suggest themselves here: first, how long will this trade remain in the hands of foreign middlemen? secondly, what are the prospects of its future? As to the former point, statistics suggest that

... but the silver itself appre-
... largely in terms of the fiat
... Japanese consumers. Cursory
... suggest that these factors should
... obviously to stimulate exports as
... depressed imports. But such was
... the case in practice. For the
... transactions were always hampered by
... that a delay of a week or even
... increase the purchasing power of
silver ... bringing about a further deprecia-
... of paper, and it was not till this element
... pernicious disturbance was removed that the
... recovered a healthy tone and grew so
... that in 1897 its volume aggregated three
... and eighty-two million *yen*, thus treading
... on the heels of the foreign commerce of
... with her three hundred million inhabi-
... and long-established international relations.

... questions of prime interest suggest them-
... here: first, how long will this trade re-
... in the hands of foreign middlemen?
... what are the prospects of its future?
... the former point, statistics suggest that

COOPERS AT WORK.

the Japanese are steadily pushing out the
foreigner. Looking at the past decade, we find
that whereas, in 1888, Japanese merchants carried on only twelve per cent of the total trade
without the intervention of foreign middlemen,
their share rose to thirty-two per cent in 1897.
It is natural, of course, that an energetic effort
should be made by the people of the country
to carry on their own commerce independently
of alien assistance. But some special features
of the foreigner's methods in Japan render his
intervention particularly irksome. Thus, in purchasing raw silk, his habit is to take the staple
into his warehouse and inspect it there at his
leisure before completing the bargain; and in
the case of tea he buys the leaf in parcels without discrimination as to their *provenance*, dumps
them all together into his firing-pans, and packs
the refired and recoloured article for export in
boxes bearing his own *cachet*. That the former
method was originally necessitated by the impossibility of trusting the Japanese to sell silk
honestly by sample, and the latter by their want
of skill to prepare the tea for Western markets,

is well understood. But if these reasons justify the foreigner's procedure, they are certainly not of a nature to appease the native's sensitiveness. The ambition of the Japanese to displace the foreign middleman must grow. Its complete gratification will be long postponed, however. The foreign resident merchant is an ideal agent. As an exporter his command of cheap capital, his experience, his knowledge of foreign markets and his connections enable him to secure prices which Japanese, working on their own account, could not obtain; as an importer he enjoys credit abroad which the Japanese are without, he pays to Japanese producers ready cash for their staples, taking upon his own shoulders all the risks of finding a sale for them beyond the sea, and he offers to Japanese consumers imports laid at their doors without any responsibility on their own part. Further, direct dealings between foreign merchants in Europe or America and Japanese merchants in Japan could not be undertaken with safety to the former. The assertion sounds harsh, but in truth Japanese traders have not yet developed the commercial conscience which is the basis of all sound business. Exceptions to this rule are numerous, of course, and their number grows steadily. But it has to be recorded, with regard, at any rate, to the Japanese coming into tradal contact with foreigners, that neither the moral sanctity of an engagement nor the material advantage of credit and confidence, nor even the practical necessity of implementing every condition of a contract, is fully appreciated by the average man of affairs.

In China there are guilds whose chief object is to strengthen credit. Lest the business of the members in general should lose the benefit of public trust, they make good the default of any one of their number. In Japan also there are guilds, but their disposition is to shield and abet the defaulter rather than to discountenance him when a foreigner is his victim. The causes chiefly responsible for this state of affairs are not difficult to analyse. One fact, constantly adduced and certainly deserving prominence, is that the Japanese frequenting the treaty ports and doing business with the foreign resident belong to a distinctly

inferior stratum of the nation. They established
their footing at a time when all contact with
foreigners was counted degrading or unpatriotic.
For the most part they were men without reputa-
tions to imperil, and they approached the foreigner
with a disposition to regard him as a person to be
neither spared nor respected. In short, they were
not, nor are they yet, fair representatives of the
upper grade of Japanese merchants. A more
subtle factor is that the wholesome atmosphere of
public opinion is virtually wanting in the region
of this open-port trade. Whatever chicanery a
Japanese may practise against foreigners, his own
version of the incident alone reaches his nationals.
Opinions may differ as to the efficacy of the checks
which the scrutiny of his fellows imposes upon the
average mortal's improbity, but that it does impose
a considerable check, none will deny. The Japanese in his dealings with foreign resident merchants is beyond the influence of such checks. If
he sins, it is with the comfortable conviction that
his sin will not find him out. Finally, there is the
broad fact that from early times trade stood in the
lowest rank of Japanese bread-winning occupa-

tions. The trader was not respected and did not respect himself. That prejudice, peculiar to a military society, has now disappeared in theory, but its practical consequences cannot be easily effaced. There is, indeed, no warrant for attributing moral deficiency to the Japanese race. If their standard of truth loses something by comparison with ours in the abstract, there is a balance of practical ingenuousness in their favour. The falsehoods covertly sanctioned by the conventions of social intercourse and every-day life in the Occident are openly permitted in Japan. Truth derives value less from its independent nobility than from the nature of its consequences. To tell the truth where to withhold or even to transform it would avert misfortune greater than the moral penalty attaching to all subterfuge, is not Japanese philosophy, any more than to obtrude personal griefs upon the notice of those whom they do not concern is a canon of Japanese courtesy. Sorrow paraded in public is either a selfish exaction of sympathy or an insincere desire to be credited with profound feeling. The truth spoken without regard for results is either the prompting of giddi-

[61]

ness or a bid for the reputation of personal
integrity at the expense of other people's happi-
ness. That is the acknowledged creed of Japan;
the partially practised but unconfessed creed of the
Occident also. But for the rest, the fibre of the
Japanese conscience seems to be just as tough
as the fibre of any other conscience, and not
more elastic. Commercial morality, however,
which is the special outgrowth of trading habits, is
still a stunted plant in Japan, and until it attains
much larger proportions the foreign middleman
will be an indispensable figure in the country's
international commerce.

We come now to the question, in what direc-
tions may the country's commerce be expected
to expand; or, speaking in broader terms, what
may be regarded as the wealth-earning capacities
of the Japan of the future? For the purposes
of such an inquiry, the first point to be determined is whether the development will be in the
production of raw materials or of manufactured
goods. The answer admits of no doubt. Japan
will always be able to send abroad considerable
quantities of silk and tea, and inconsiderable

quantities of marine products,[1] copper, coal,[2] camphor, sulphur, rice and minor staples; but with regard to these, either her producing capacity is inelastic or her market is limited. It is certain, indeed, that she will by and by have to look abroad for supplies of the necessaries of life. Rice is the staple diet of her people, and she seems to have almost reached the potential maximum of her rice-growing area; for in spite of her genial climate and seemingly fertile soil, the extent of her arable land is disproportionately small. She has only eleven and one half millions of acres under crops, and there is no prospect of any large extension, or of the yields being improved by new agricultural processes. The Japanese farmer understands his work thoroughly. His competence is sufficiently proved when we

[1] Japan's fishing industry is doubtless capable of great development. She has 17,602 miles of coast and 270,000 families devoted to fishing, or more than 15 families to each mile. They employ 330,706 boats, and 1,194,408 nets, representing a capital of about twenty-eight million *yen*, and the total value of the annual catch is put at forty-eight million *yen*, though one hundred millions would probably be nearer the truth. The fishermen are sturdy, courageous fellows, but their methods are primitive, and virtually no improvements have yet been introduced.

[2] It was at one time supposed that Japan possessed great mineral wealth, but experience has corrected the impression. The output of her various mines increases steadily, it is true, but its total annual value does not exceed thirty million *yen*.

say that by the skilful use of fertilisers he has been able to raise good crops of rice on the same land during fifteen or twenty centuries. On the other hand, not only is the population increasing rapidly, but in proportion to the growth of general prosperity and the distribution of wealth the lower classes of the people, who used formerly to be content with barley and millet, now regard rice as an essential article of food. It cannot be long, therefore, before large supplies of this cereal will have to be drawn from abroad. The same is true of timber, which has already become inconveniently scarce. Japan cannot even grow her own cotton, and nature has not fitted her pastures for sheep; so that materials for her people's clothing have all to be imported. Her future lies undoubtedly in industrial enterprise. She has an abundance of cheap labour and her people are exceptionally gifted with intelligence, docility, manual dexterity and artistic taste. Everything points to a great future for them as manufacturers. This is not a matter of mere conjecture. Striking practical evidence has already been furnished. Cotton spinning may

A MOUNTAIN CREEK

JAPAN

...and use of ... ...
...al crops ... ...
...or twenty ... ...
...t only is the pr... ... ...
...in proportion ...
...erty and the distribution ... wealth
...esses of the people, ...
...and with body and ... ...
...an essential ... ... Increasing, therefore, ... supplies of
...vail have to be ... ... considered.
...is true of cotton which has already
...nce into this sense. Japan cannot
grow her own ... and nature has not
...her possessed ... ... so that materials
...have to be imported.
...with industrial enter-
...ce of cheap labour and
...fully gifted with intel-
...and dexterity and artistic
...to a great future for
...manufacture. This is not a matter
...but actual practical evidence
...furnished. Cotton spinning may

A MOUNTAIN CHAIR.

be specially referred to. As long ago as 1862, the feudal chief of Satsuma started a mill with five thousand spindles in his fief, but during a whole decade he found only one imitator. In 1882, however, a year which may be regarded as the opening of Japan's industrial era, this enterprise began to attract capital, and in the course of four years fifteen mills were established working fifty-five thousand spindles. By foreign observers this new departure was regarded with contemptuous amusement. The Japanese were declared to be without organising capacity, incapable of sustained energy and generally unfitted for factory work. These desponding views had soon to be radically modified, for by 1897 the number of mills had increased to sixty-three, the number of spindles to some eight hundred thousand, the capital invested to twenty-one million *yen*, and the average annual profit per spindle was three and one half *yen*, or thirteen and one third per cent on the capital. The rapidity of this development suggests unsoundness, but speed is a marked characteristic of Japan's modern progress. In 1880, for example, a man named Isozaki of Okayama prefecture carried to Kobe a specimen of a new kind of floor-mat, the outcome of two years' thought and trial. Briefly described, it was matting with a weft of fine green reeds and a warp of cotton yarn, having a coloured design woven into it. Isozaki found difficulty in getting any one to test the salability of his invention by sending it abroad. Sixteen years later, the "brocade matting" industry of Okayama prefecture alone occupied seven hundred and thirty-four weaving establishments with nine thousand and eighty-five stands of looms, gave employment to nine thousand three hundred and fifty-seven artisans, of whom five thousand three hundred and thirty-five were females, and turned out two and one quarter million *yen* worth of this pretty floor covering. Meanwhile, the total value of the industry's output throughout the empire had reached nearly six million *yen*, and the quantity exported stood at three millions, approximately, in the customs returns. Here, then, is a trade which rose from nothing to a position of great importance in sixteen years. Even more remarkable in some respects has been the development of the textile industry. In 1886 the total production of silk and cotton fabrics was eighteen million *yen;* ten years later it had increased to ninety-six millions,[1] the number of weaving establishments being six hundred and sixty thousand four hundred and eighty, the number of looms nine hundred and thirty-nine thousand one hundred and twenty-three, and the number of operatives one million forty-two thousand eight hundred and sixty-six, of whom nine hundred and eighty-five thousand three hundred and sixteen were females. The manufacture of lucifer matches is another industry of entirely recent growth. A few years ago Japan used to import all the matches she needed, but by 1897 she was able not only to

---

[1] The Japanese have been skilled weavers for many centuries, but a great impetus was given to this enterprise by the introduction of improved machinery and the use of aniline dyes after the opening of the country to foreign intercourse. Indigo has always been the staple dye-stuff of the country. Twenty million *yen* worth is produced annually. But for colours other than blue and its various tones, aniline dyes are now imported to the extent of one and one quarter million *yen* yearly. The growth of the textile industry has also been greatly stimulated by the introduction of cotton yarns of fine and uniform quality. Formerly all cotton cloths were woven out of coarse, irregular, hand-spun yarns, so that nothing like regularity of weight and texture could be secured. It thus appears that Japan owes the remarkable development of her textile industry to foreign intercourse.

supply her own wants but also to send abroad five and one half million *yen* worth. Without carrying these statistics to wearisome length, we may confine ourselves to noting that in six branches of manufacturing industry which may be said to have been called into active existence by the opening of the country — namely, silk and cotton fabrics, cotton yarns, matches, fancy matting and straw braid — Japan's exports in 1888 aggregated only three and one quarter million *yen*, whereas the corresponding figure for 1897 was forty-two and one quarter millions. In short, the export increased thirteen hundred per cent in a decade.

With such results before us, it is impossible to doubt that Japan has a great manufacturing future. The fact has, indeed, been partially recognised and much talked of within the past few years, especially in the United States, where the prospect of Japanese industrial competition was recently presented to the public in almost alarming proportions. On the other hand, among foreigners resident in Japan the general estimate of native manufacturing capacity is low. Doubtless, as is usually the case, the truth lies be-

LANTERN MAKERS.

tween the two extremes. Japanese industrial competition will be a formidable fact one of these days, but the time is still distant. Progress is checked by one manifest obstacle, — defective integrity. Concerning every industry whose products have found a place in the catalogue of modern Japan's exports, the same story has to be told: just as really substantial development seemed about to be obtained, fraudulent adulteration or dishonestly careless technique interfered to destroy credit and disgust the foreign consumer. The Japanese deny that the whole responsibility for these disastrous moral *laches* rests with them. The treaty-port middleman, they say, buys so thriftily that high-quality goods cannot be supplied to him. That excuse may be partially valid, but it is certainly not exhaustive. The vital importance of establishing and maintaining the reputation of an article offered newly in markets where it has to compete with rivals of old-established excellence is not yet fully appreciated in Japan. As to organising capacity, the possession of which by the Japanese has been strenuously doubted by

[69]

more than one foreign critic, there are proofs more weighty than any theories. In the cotton-spinning industry, for example, the Japanese are brought into direct competition in their own markets with Indian mills, employing cheap native labour, organised and managed by Englishmen and having the raw material at their doors. The victory rests with the Japanese, from which it may fairly be inferred that their organisation is not specially defective or their method costly.[1] Yet there is one consideration that must not be lost sight of. It is the inexperience of the Japanese — their lack of standards. Japan is dressing herself in a material civilisation that was made to the measure of alien nations, and curious misfits are inevitably developed in the process. If the England of 1837, for example, — that is to say, England as she was at the commencement of the Victorian era, — could have been suddenly projected forward to 1897 and invited to adapt herself to

---

[1] Japanese mills are kept at work twenty-three hours out of the twenty-four with one shift of operatives, and their production per spindle is forty per cent greater than the production at Bombay mills and nearly double of the production at English mills.

[70]

the moral and material conditions of the latter period, the task, though almost inconceivably difficult, would have been far easier than that which Japan set herself twenty-five years ago, for England would at least have possessed the preliminary training, the habit of mind and the trend of intelligence, all of which were wanting to Japan. That essential difference should be easy to remember, yet it is constantly forgotten by observers of Japan's progress. Again and again they make the mistake of measuring her acts by the standards to which they have themselves been educated. Again and again they fall into the error of deducing from her failures and perplexities the same inferences that similar perplexities and failures would suggest in Europe or America.

If the citizens of Tokyo hesitate to spend large sums upon street repair, they are accused of blind parsimony, though the fact is that, never having had any practical knowledge of really fine roadways, they have not yet learned to appreciate them. If Japanese officials do not at once succeed in solving the very difficult

[71]

problem of Formosan administration, it is concluded that they lack administrative ability, though absolute lack of experience suffices to account for their ill-success. If the people have not yet made any significant contribution to the sum of Occidental scientific knowledge or mechanical contrivances, they are dismissed as imitative, not initiative; which is much as though we should charge a lad with want of originality because, having barely mastered the integral calculus, he did not write some new chapters on quaternions. If they have not yet reduced constitutional government to a smoothly working system, have not yet emerged from a confusion of political coteries into the orderly condition of two great parties each capable of assuming and discharging administrative responsibilities, they are declared unfit for representative institutions, though they have tried them for only six years after fifteen centuries of military feudalism or hereditary oligarchy. If they do not carry on their new industries with the minimum of efficient labour, and if they fail to appreciate the economical necessity of bestowing constant care

upon the machinery and seeking to rise above first results, instead of regarding them as the *ne plus ultra* of subsequent achievement, they are pronounced radically deficient in the industrial instinct, whereas the truth is that they have not as yet any accurate perception of the standards which experience and competition have established in foreign countries. The condition of their army and of their navy shows that not capacity but practice is what the Japanese lack. These two services are altogether modern creations. Cursory students of Japanese history rise from the perusal with a conviction that they have been reading the records of an essentially military race, and that good weapons alone are needed to make good soldiers of such people. But if the history of ancient and mediæval Japan teaches anything, its lesson is that the martial *morale* could formerly be claimed for only a very small section of the Japanese nation. The *Samurai* class numbered three millions among forty, less than one thirteenth of the total population, and to the *Samurai* class were confined the privilege of carrying swords

[73]

and all the honour and distinctions attaching to
that badge of aristocracy from the very beginning of the nation's social organisation. The
peasant, the artisan and the trader were crushed
under the armed heel of the soldier, and if long
centuries of enforced and confessed inferiority
and contemptuous seclusion from camp and
court have any injurious influence upon the
spirit of virility and self-respect, the Japanese
people, as a whole, should have been found conspicuously lacking in that spirit when the feudal
system fell and the traditional distinctions of
caste were abolished at the beginning of the
Meiji era. It was, nevertheless, from the mass
of the people, not from the *Samurai*, that the
rank and file of the army and navy had to be
taken after the Restoration. The new conscrip-
tion law paid no attention to the social distinctions rigidly observed under the feudal regimen.
The three despised classes — the farmers, the
mechanics and the merchants — found themselves
suddenly required to bear arms and to discharge
duties for which they had been taught to believe themselves morally incompetent. None of

the daring enterprises essayed by the makers of
modern Japan attracted more interest than this
reversal of the conditions which had hitherto
been regarded as the bases of Japanese society—
this appeal to the plebeian to enter the field
specially reserved to the patrician during fifteen
centuries. Could the new system work? Could
a trustworthy *personnel* for the army and navy
be obtained from such materials? While these
questions were still fresh upon men's lips they
were answered by a rude and conclusive test.
Five years after the demise of feudalism a rebellion broke out in the south of Japan, and
the regiments of conscripts had to be pitted
against the very *élite* of the Japanese *Samurai*,
—the two-sworded men of Satsuma. The astonishing results were that the rustic and the
city clerk showed themselves almost as good
fighters as the *Samurai*, and the government
demonstrated that it had been able to organise
an army after Western models, and that its
officers could conduct a campaign in accordance
with the rules of Western strategy and tactics.
Seventeen years later, Japan entering the field

[75]

against China furnished a conclusive proof of
the excellence of her military organisation. She
had to undertake the most difficult task that
falls to the lot of a belligerent, — the task of
sending over sea two *corps d'armée* (aggregating
a hundred and twenty thousand men) and
maintaining them for several months in widely
separated fields — one in eastern and central
Manchuria, the other in the Liaotung peninsula
and subsequently in Shantung province. The
effort did not appear to embarrass her. There
was no sign of confusion or perplexity; no
breakdown of the commissariat or transport arrangements; no failure of the ambulance or
hospital service. Everything worked smoothly,
and the public were compelled to recognise that
Japan had not only elaborated a very efficient
piece of military mechanism, but also developed
ability to employ it to the best advantage. The
same inference was suggested by her navy.
Although during two and a half centuries her
people had been debarred by arbitrary legislation from navigating the high seas, the twenty-
fifth year after the repeal of these crippling laws

... ... furnished a conclusive proof of
... ... of her military organisation. She
... to undertake the most difficult task that
... ... of a belligerent,—the task of
... ... sea two *corps d'armée* (aggregating
... ... and twenty thousand men) and
... ... them for several months in widely
... ... districts—one in eastern and central
... ..., the other in the Liaotung peninsula
and subsequently in Shantung province. The
effort did not appear to embarrass her. There
was no sign of confusion or perplexity; no
breakdown of the commissariat or transport or
equipments; no failure of the ambulance or
hospital service. Everything worked smoothly,
and the public were compelled to recognise that
Japan had not only elaborated a very efficient
piece of military mechanism, but also developed
ability to employ it to the best advantage. The
same inference was suggested by her navy.
Although during two and a half centuries her
people had been debarred by arbitrary legislation from navigating the high seas, the twenty-
nith year after the repeal of these crippling laws

PRIVATE RESIDENCE ON THE BLUFF AT YOKOHAMA.

saw the State in possession of a squadron of thirty-three serviceable ships of war, officered and manned solely by the Japanese, constantly manœuvring in distant waters without accident, and evidently possessing all the qualities of a fine fighting force. In the war with China (1894–95) this navy showed its capacity by destroying or capturing, without the loss of a single ship, the whole of the enemy's fleet, whereas the latter's superiority in armour and armament ought to have produced a very different issue. It may be noted here, although the fact is foreign to our immediate subject, that for all military or naval purposes Japan possesses an immense advantage over China.

The Japanese *Samurai* is an ideal officer. Hardy, intelligent, fearless, ready to share the privations of his men and to abandon to them all the merit of victory, with little taste for luxury, a strong sense of duty and absolute devotion to his profession, he has all the qualities of a successful leader. China is entirely without such men. Even if the mass of her people could be imbued with the strong, almost fanatical,

[77]

spirit of patriotism that is now known to fire
the commonest Japanese, making him willing
to sacrifice his life at any moment for king and
country, she would still lack the traditions which
in Japan exalt the profession of arms above
all other occupations, and the instincts
that distinguish the *Samurai* type. But
whatever allowance be made on account of the
splendid material furnished by the *Samurai*
class for officering an army and a navy, the
general fact remains that the Japanese, using
the plebeian classes for rank and file, have carried
the two services to a state of the highest organisation, and have proved that they can assimilate
not merely the forms but also the spirit of
foreign systems. On the other hand, a visit
to their factories shows machinery treated care-
lessly, employees so numerous that they impede
rather than expedite business, and a general lack
of the precision, regularity and earnestness that
characterise successful industrial enterprises in
Europe and America. Achievement in one
direction and comparative failure in another,
whereas the factors making for success are

similar in each, indicates, not incapacity in the latter case, but defects of standard and experience. The vast majority of the Japanese have no adequate conception of what is meant by a highly organised industrial or commercial enterprise. They have never made the practical acquaintance of anything of the kind, nor ever breathed a pure business atmosphere. For elaborating their military and naval systems they had close access to foreign models, every detail of which could be carefully scrutinised, and they availed themselves freely of the assistance of foreign experts, French, German and British. But in the field of manufacture and trade their inspection of foreign models is necessarily superficial, and they are without the coöperation of foreign experts. It may be supposed that, since the foreign middleman plays such an important part in the country's over-sea commerce, his skill and experience must have been equally available for the purposes of industrial enterprise. But two difficulties stood in the way; one legal, the other sentimental. The treaties forbade foreigners to hold real estate or engage

[79]

in business outside the limits of the settlements, thus rendering it impossible for them either to start factories on their own account or to enter into partnership with native industrials; and an almost morbid anxiety to prove their independent competence impelled the Japanese to dispense prematurely with the services of foreign employees. Rapid as has been the country's material progress, it might have been at once quicker and sounder had these restrictive treaties been revised a dozen years earlier, when Japan was still upon the threshold of her manufacturing career, and before repeated failures to obtain considerate treatment at the hands of Western Powers had prejudiced her against foreigners in all capacities. In 1885 she was ready to welcome the Occidental to every part of the country; regarded it as a matter of course that he should own real estate, and would gladly have become his partner in commerce or manufacture. In 1895 she had come to suspect that closer association with him might have dangers and disadvantages, and that the soil of Japan ought to be preserved from falling into his possession.

... ents,

... er to

to enter

... s; and

their inde-

Japanese to

... ga

... ntry's

... ce

... s

... Japan

... anufactures

... s to obtain

... of Western

... st foreigners

... ready to

... part of the

... course that

... ll gladly have

... ace ! ... or manufacture

In 18.. ... that closer

associa... ... have dangers and

disadv... gs, and that the soil of Japan ought

to be preserved from ... ing into his possession

WATER-CARRIER FILLING HIS PAILS AT A WELL IN A SIDE STREET IN KYOTO.

ATTITUDE: FOREIGN RESIDENTS

There are evidences that this mood, so injurious to her own interests, is being replaced by more liberal sentiments; but in the meanwhile she has been induced to stand aloof from alien aids at a time when they might have profited her immensely, and to struggle without guidance toward standards of which she has as yet only a dim perception. Already, too, some of the advantages of cheap labour and inexpensive living are disappearing, and, on the whole, there seems to be little doubt that though great manufacturing successes lie before her, she will take many years to realise them.

XXII

MODERN JAPAN

IT IS IMPOSSIBLE, OF course, to form any clear idea of Japan's condition and prospects without some knowledge of her public finances. The subject can be discussed without making any large demand on the reader's patience.

Under the feudal system the whole of the land in the empire was regarded as the property of the State and parcelled out into two hundred and seventy-seven fiefs, great and small, which were assigned to as many nobles. These held the land in trust and were empowered to derive revenue from it on the basis of one half of the produce to the feudal chief, one half to the farmer. The latter was only a tenant. He had no title to the soil he tilled and might not transfer it. But he generally received considerate treatment from the officers of the fief, and could count on almost absolute fixity of tenure. In practice it was found convenient to collect the revenues of the fiefs in the form of rice only, leaving the other crops entirely to the farmer. Thus the whole burden being thrown on the rice crop, the proportion of half to the feudatory and half to the farmer did not hold in the case of that cereal. Out of a total production of one hundred and fifty-three million bushels, the portion delivered for the support of the nobles and their retainers aggregated one hundred and twelve million bushels annually, the money value of which at the time of the Restoration (1867) was one hundred and sixty-five million *yen*.[1] The fiefs having been handed back to the sovereign in 1871, it was decided to provide for the feudal nobles and the *Samurai* in general by the payment of lump sums in commutation or by handing to them public bonds the interest on which should constitute a source of income. The result of this transaction, into the details of

---

[1] The *yen* of these calculations is the present unit of Japanese currency — a coin worth fifty gold cents (two shillings), approximately.

which we need not enter, was that bonds having a total face value of one hundred and ninety-one and a half million *yen* were issued, and ready-money payments aggregating twenty-one and a quarter million *yen* were made. This was the foundation of Japan's national debt. Indeed these public bonds aggregating one hundred and ninety-one and a half million *yen* may be said to represent the bulk of the State's liabilities during the first twenty-five years of the *Meiji* period. The government had also to take over the debts of the fiefs, amounting to thirty-one million *yen*, of which twenty-one and a half millions were paid with interest-bearing bonds, the remainder with ready money. If to the above figures we add two foreign loans aggregating sixteen and a half million *yen* (now completely repaid), a loan of fifteen million *yen* incurred on account of the only serious rebellion that marked the passage from the old to the new *régime*, — the Satsuma revolt of 1877, — loans of thirty-three million *yen* for public works, thirteen million *yen* for naval construction and fourteen and a half millions in connection with the fiat currency, we

JAPANESE CARPENTERS AT WORK.

have a total of three hundred and five million *yen*, being the whole national debt of Japan during the first twenty years of her new era under Imperial administration.

We need not further examine the origin and early history of the country's debt. The story is sufficiently set forth in the above figures. Let us pass at once then to the great epoch of Japanese finance — the war with China in 1894–95. The direct expenditures on account of the war aggregated two hundred and forty million *yen*, of which total one hundred and thirty-five millions were added to the national debt, the remainder being defrayed with accumulations of surplus revenue, with a part of the indemnity received from China and with voluntary contributions from patriotic subjects. In the immediate sequel of the war the government elaborated a large programme of armament expansion and public works. The army at the time of the war consisted of six divisions and the Imperial guards, with a peace establishment of seventy thousand and a war strength of two hundred and sixty-eight thousand ; the navy of thirty-three vessels, exclusive of twenty-six torpedo boats, representing a displacement of sixty-three thousand tons. It was resolved to raise the number of divisions to twelve, with a peace establishment of one hundred and forty-five thousand and a war strength of five hundred and sixty thousand, and the navy to sixty-seven ships (besides eleven torpedo catchers and one hundred and fifteen torpedo boats) with an aggregate displacement of two hundred and fifty-eight thousand tons. The expenditures for these unproductive purposes as well as for coast fortifications, dockyards, and so on, came to three hundred and twenty-five million *yen*, and the total of the productive expenditures included in the programme was one hundred and ninety million *yen;* namely, one hundred and twenty millions for railways, telegraphs and telephones, twenty millions for riparian improvements, twenty millions in aid of industrial and agricultural banks and so forth; the whole programme thus involving an outlay of five hundred and fifteen million *yen*. To meet this large figure the Chinese indemnity and other assets furnished three hundred millions, and it was decided that the remaining two hundred and fifteen millions should be obtained by domestic loans, the programme to be carried completely into operation, with trifling exceptions, by the year 1905. This somewhat wearisome array of figures may be concluded by adding that Japan's total indebtedness was, before the outbreak of the present war, five hundred and sixty-five million *yen* in round numbers ; and that the amount has since been increased once by a foreign loan and twice by domestic loans.

Having now obtained a clear idea of the State's liabilities, we pass to consider briefly its assets. The public revenue is remarkably small when viewed with regard to the population (forty-six and a half millions) and to the career of vigorous progress upon which the country has embarked. During the fiscal year of 1903–1904 only two hundred and fifty-one million *yen* came into the treasury, one hundred and forty-one and a half millions of which represented direct taxes, being at the rate of three *yen* (one dollar and fifty cents) per head of the population.

JAPAN

The question at once arises, how can a country maintaining an army of over half a million men and a navy of sixty-seven ships, hope to pay its way with an annual income of one hundred and twenty-five million dollars? The feat presents an impossible aspect to Western financiers. But we have to note that a little money goes a long way in Japan. Her army, for example, required in 1903–1904 an annual outlay of only thirty-eight and a half million *yen*, and twenty-two millions sufficed for the navy. No other country supports such establishments at such a petty cost. Considering, however, the increasing cost of armament expansion and productive public works mapped out in the immediate sequel of the war with China, it often appeared that the State would soon be confronted with a considerable deficiency of revenue. This question, though its outlines have been but vaguely appreciated, has often caused considerable uneasiness in Japan and evoked pessimistic criticisms abroad. A very brief examination will show that no grounds exist for uneasiness. Omitting minor items of expanding income —

. . . . . . N

. . . . . . how can a com-
. . . over half a million
. . . ships, hope to
. . . . of one hun-
. . . . . Fast? The feat
. . . . Western fron-
. . . . a little money
. . . . army, for ex-
. . . an annual outlay
. . . . affoat *yen*, and
. . . . the navy. No
. . . establishments at
. . . . however, the in-
. . . . dom and pro-
. . . . . out in the
. . . . China, is often
. . . . an be confronted
a . . . . of revenue. This
. . . . s have been but
. . . . often caused consider-
. . . . town and evoked pessimistic
. . . . . . abroad. A very brief examination will
. . . . that no grounds exist for uneasiness.
. . . . . minor items of expanding income—

A STREET IN ENOSHIMA.

such as a steady growth of the receipts from state railways, posts and telegraphs; an addition of fully seven million *yen* from customs duties under the new tariff, and so forth — there is the general fact that a large reserve of taxable capacity exists. It has been shown above that the farmers formerly paid to their immediate landlords, the feudal nobles, fully two thirds of the rice crop, which payment represented rent and taxes. When feudalism fell (in 1871) the nobles ceased to stand between the sovereign owner of the soil and the agricultural classes that tilled it. The Emperor then took a remarkable step. He conferred on the farmers, who had hitherto been mere tenants, the right of permanent possession, in consideration of a perpetual annual payment nominally representing two and a half per cent of the market value of the land, but in reality amounting to less than one and a quarter per cent. The result was that eleven million acres of land became the property of the farmers without the disbursement of any purchase money on their part, their sole liability being a yearly payment of three and a half *yen* (one dollar and seventy-five cents) per acre. It is to this payment that the name of "land tax" is now given; a misleading term, since it conceals the fact that rent also is included in the sum. The average rice crop at present is two hundred million bushels, and if two thirds of it were paid into the treasury, as was the case in feudal times, the resulting revenue derived by the State from the land would be about two hundred and sixty-five million *yen*, whereas it was in 1903–1904 only less than forty-seven millions under the present system. In short, the landholder pays about eighteen per cent of what he paid formerly, and he owns the land into the bargain. It does not appear that he fared very badly under the old system, and certainly, judging from past experience, there can be no doubt of his ability to contribute much more liberally to the public revenue than he does at present. But there is great reluctance to make any additional demand on the agriculturist. Taxation in former times signified solely the payments made by farmers. Mechanics and tradesmen were not regularly

taxed. The system would have been exactly
that of the "single tax" had not the urban lands
escaped, as they do still escape, with a most un-
justly small impost. Hence to reduce taxation
meant, in practice, to abate the agriculturists'
contributions; and inasmuch as the Emperor
promised to lighten the people's burdens after
the abolition of feudalism, his pledge was held
to have been addressed direct to landholders.
Thus a sentimental notion exists that immunity
has been imperially guaranteed to tillers of the
soil, and no cabinet nor any political party cares
to imperil its popularity by declaring for an increase of the land tax. The facts, however, cannot be gainsaid, and by and by the present
romantic mood will yield to plain expediency.
Then there are the taxes upon alcoholic bever-
ages, upon tobacco, and upon other commodities
or industries, as well as upon incomes. It is a
great misconception to speak of the Japanese as
heavily taxed. The fact is that for the past
three decades or more they have been accus-
tomed to taxes so light that they cannot easily
reconcile themselves now to the prospect of a

less agreeable state of affairs. Still timid in
their ideas of finance, they have not fully realised
that their new status imposes a greatly altered
scale of national expenditure. But the ability to
contribute much more liberally to the funds of
the State than they do at present certainly exists, and can be invoked at any time.

The great difficulty under which Japan labours
is want of capital. Statistics show that the
capital actually engaged in economic enterprises
was, in 1902, nearly eight hundred and seventy-
nine million *yen*, and that two hundred and
forty-eight more millions were pledged, though
not yet paid up. On the other hand, the
volume of circulating media was in 1903 only
four hundred and twelve and a half million
yen,[1] and the funds at the disposal of the banks
amounted to five hundred and twenty-five
millions. Recourse to foreign capital would

[1] That is to say, a little less than nine *yen* per head of the population.
It is interesting to note the corresponding figures in Occidental countries ;
thus : Austria, eighteen *yen;* Denmark, twenty-four ; France, seventy-
eight ; Germany, thirty-nine ; the United Kingdom, thirty-seven ; the
United States, fifty-nine. There has been much talk on the part of
superficial Japanese and foreign critics about an excessive volume of
currency in Japan, but it will be seen from the above figures that the
contention is quite baseless.

be the natural plan under such circumstances, but, as already explained, so long as she was a silver-using country, Japan hesitated to contract gold debts, and the capitalists of Europe or America would of course have insisted that all loans should be on a gold basis. It was chiefly with the object of removing this obstacle that Japanese financiers decided, in 1897, to adopt the gold standard. They hoped that their five-per-cent public bonds would thus become readily salable in the markets of Europe and America. But Europe and America have not yet acquired full confidence in Japanese finance, and, moreover, the bonds themselves present some features not unlikely to deter foreign investors. The day is probably not far distant when Japanese securities will become favourite investments abroad. Meanwhile there is certainly a great opening for foreign capital in the field of industrial enterprise. An examination of the returns of sixty-eight joint-stock companies for the second half of 1897 shows that they paid an average dividend of sixteen and an eighth per cent, and it is not to be doubted that still better results

could be attained were foreign business experience and cheap capital available.

One of the paradoxes of modern Japan's story
is that her political advance has proved a barrier
to her material progress. In the great national
fermentation that inaugurated the *Meiji* era,
the State's best men rose to the surface, and
had it been possible to leave the reins of government permanently in their hands, a steady
march along all lines of sound development
would have been assured. But it was not
possible. Parliamentary government had to
come, bringing with it all the confusion of multitudinous counsels and the clashing of party
politics. Let us trace the record briefly.

No one reading Japanese history carefully can
fail to infer that representative institutions are
in the genius of the nation. From the very
earliest eras the sovereign ceased to be autocratic. All the highest offices of State became
the hereditary possessions of certain great
families, and as generation followed generation
each unit of this oligarchy of households attained
the dimensions of a clan. By and by the ex-

igencies of the times gave birth to a military
aristocracy, headed by a generalissimo (*Shogun*),
into whose hands the administrative authority
passed. But even in this military feudalism no
traces of genuine autocracy are found. Just
as the extensive powers nominally vested in
the central figure, the *Shogun*, were in reality
wielded by a large body of ministers and coun-
cillors, so the local autonomy enjoyed by each
fief was exercised, not by the chief himself, but
by his leading vassals. A united effort on the
part of all the clans to overthrow such a system
and wrest the administrative power from the
Shogun could have only one logical outcome,
the combined exercise of the recovered power
by those who had been instrumental in recover-
ing it. There was no open enunciation of such
a principle, but it could be read clearly enough
on the face of events and between the lines of
the oath sworn by the Emperor when he placed
himself once again at the head of civil affairs in
1867 — the oath that "wide counsels should be
sought and all things determined by public discussion." It is plain that to fulfil this promise a

representative assembly must be convened. But when ? Some preparations were indispensable, and after a time the nation began to suspect that the preparatory interval was being unduly prolonged in the interests of the clique of statesmen whom the Restoration had brought into office, the leading clansmen of Satsuma and Choshiu. At first the suspicion found only vague expression, but by degrees it grew into a dread, partly genuine, partly factitious, that two or three great clans were seeking to climb into permanent power on the ruins of feudalism. A clamour against *Sat-Cho* (Satsuma and Choshiu) cabinets then (1878) began to be audible, and found a mouthpiece in a now celebrated politician, Count Itagaki, who had seceded three years previously from the ranks of the Restoration statesmen for reasons that need not concern the reader. At the time of his secession his love of liberty had not hardened into a political platform. That came a little later, and with it came occupants of the platform — a few who had been in office and wanted to repeat the experience, a greater number who had never been in office and wanted

... to conceal ...
... were indispensable, and
... reason to suspect that the
... being unduly prolonged
... of statesmen whom
... into office, the
... and Choshiu. At
... by some expression.
... a deceit, partly
... two or three great
... into permanent
... ositicism. A clamour
... and Choshiu) cabinets
... and found a
... coalition, Count
... years previously
... ation of such for
... the reader. At
... his love of liberty had
... political platform. The
... with it came occupants
... who had been in office
... experience, a good
... in office and went

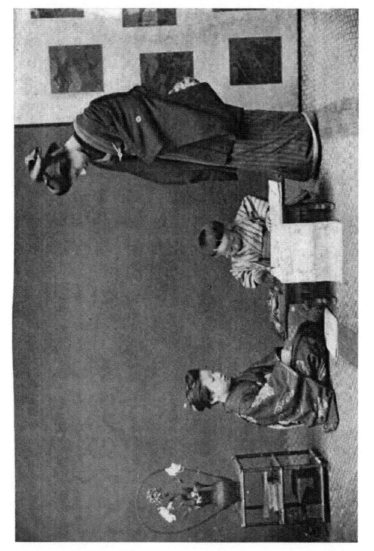

LEARNING TO WRITE.

to try the experience, and a still greater number who wanted freedom of speech and representative institutions. Thus the Liberal party (*Jiyu-to*) was organised, the first political association of modern Japan. Three years later (1881) another notable secession from the ranks of officialdom took place. The seceder was Count Okuma. He, too, wanted representative institutions, but he wanted them at once. That was the chief difference between him and Count Itagaki. The latter laboured for the principle, the former for its immediate practical application. It may be supposed that the two would thenceforth have joined hands, and indeed, so far as theory was concerned, nothing held them apart. But officially they were enemies. Itagaki seceded in 1875 and formed his party in 1878. Okuma seceded in 1881 and formed his party at once. Thus Okuma had remained for six years a member of the cabinet that threw off Itagaki, and in his capacity of minister had during that time been privy to sundry severe measures for the restraint of Itagaki's agitation. So the two men, though working for the same purpose with similar instruments, could not join forces. Okuma called his followers the Progressists, a term well adapted to the circumstances of the party's birth.

These names deserve notice. They afford a clew to one of the chief obstacles standing in the way of the consummation of representative institutions — party government. It is plain that a true Progressist must be a Liberal, and a true Liberal a Progressist. The terms are distinctive only; they do not indicate any difference of platforms. There is, in fact, no difference and there can be no difference. The Japan of to-day is permeated from head to foot by the spirit of progress. If a rare conservative survive here and there, he has not strength to make his existence practically noticeable. Parties are grouped about persons, not about principles. It is thus inevitable that their elements should lack cohesion and be always subject to disintegrating influences. Another difficulty, more remediable, but for the moment not less serious, is that no party has yet succeeded in permanently attaching to itself any considerable number of the statesmen whose experience indi-

cates them as the natural and indeed the only
trustworthy managers of State affairs. That is a
point demanding brief explanation, for to Anglo-
Saxon readers it will appear scarcely comprehen-
sible that statesmen and politicians should be
grouped in different camps. The records of
England's pre-Victorian struggle for party government shows us a king on one side, clinging to his
traditional prerogative; a parliament and its
leaders on the other, fighting against subservience
to the royal mandate. But in Japan the contest
has always been between officialdom and non-
officialdom. At the Restoration in 1867, as has
been already noted, a group of the most brilliant
and competent men in the empire got the administrative reins into their hands and held them for
twenty-four years. At first they were virtually
unopposed. A few adversaries might have been
found among lovers of the old order; but these
had no strength to raise their heads, and were,
moreover, hopelessly out of touch with the time.
By degrees, however, the vast hotchpotch of
changes and reforms introduced by the hands of
eager statesmen became a dish too varied to suit

the palate of all. Now by this measure, now by that, tastes were differentiated, and unit after unit of the administrative coterie drifted into opposition. A few had recourse to force, and fell in battle or under the headsman's sword. But, with these few exceptions, peaceable opposition was the programme of the seceders. They were, in fact, advocates of constitutional government, and they endeavoured to limit their advocacy to constitutional methods. Foremost among them were the two spoken of above, Counts Itagaki and Okuma. These men alone need be considered in connection with the growth of political parties ; their figures dwarf all the rest. Count Itagaki is the Rousseau of Japan. A passionate lover of liberty in the abstract, he does not concern himself deeply about the concrete applications of his principles. Count Okuma may be compared in some respects to Sir Robert Peel. To remarkable financial ability and a lucid, vigorous judgment he adds the faculty of placing himself on the crest of any wave that a genuine *aura popularis* has begun to swell. Japanese political parties are often spoken of by foreign observers as something quite beyond ordinary com-

. . . measures, now by
. . . and act after well
. . . noted in opposition.
. . . and fell in battle or
. . . But with these few
. . . tion was the pro
. . . . . They were, in fact,
. . . . government, and they
. . . made easy to contain
. . . . . among them were the
. . . . . Itagaki and Okuma,
. . . . . combined in connection
. . . . political parties; their figures
. . . . Count Itagaki is the Rousseau
. . . Japan. A passionate lover of liberty in the
. . . it, he does not concern himself deeply about
. . . the application of its principles. Count
. . . may be compared in some respects to Sir
. . . Peel. His remarkable financial ability and
. . . . . judgment, he holds the loyalty of
. . . self on the crest of any wave that a
. . . popularity has begun to swell. Japan-
. . . professes no prejudice of this kind by foreign
. . . something quite beyond ordinary com-

VILLAGE OF KIGA, NEAR MIYANOSHITA.

prehension. But the story of their evolution presents no real difficulty. The two here mentioned — Liberals and Progressists — are the only associations of the kind that need be seriously considered by the student. Cabals have been formed within their ranks and independent coteries outside, the occasional result being a welter of factions, bewildering and disheartening. But such things represent the incidental struggles of the moment, not the guiding principles of the era. Officialdom stood arrayed against the parties; officialdom under the leadership of the Restoration statesmen, with whom were allied the army officered chiefly by Choshiu men, and the navy officered chiefly by Satsuma men. On one side, two strong bodies of political agitators struggling to obtain the practical fulfilment of the Emperor's promise; on the other, the Sat-Cho holders of office and all their official followers, struggling to postpone that consummation, — such was the spectacle presented to the nation. It might easily have become a dangerous spectacle, but the government paralysed its elements of commotion by proclaiming (in 1881) that a constitution should

be issued in 1890 and a Diet convened in 1891.
Thenceforth the parties could only wait. The
framer of the constitution was Marquis Ito. These
titles, "Marquis," "Count," "Viscount," must not
be taken as indicating that the makers of Japan's
modern history belonged to the ancient nobility of
Japan. Marquis Ito was plain Mr. Ito when he
first appeared upon the political stage, and the
same is true of Okuma, Inouye, Itagaki, Kido,
Saigo, and so on; in short, of nearly the whole
group of brilliant publicists who led Japan from
the old to the new and steered her through all her
subsequent difficulties. Many of them can look
back to strange and stirring experiences since the
days when, as feudal retainers, with no foundations
for fortune-building except high courage and keen
intelligence, they laid plans that must have
seemed at the moment idle dreams, but were destined to raise the country to an unlooked-for place
among the nations, and themselves to heights of
influence and fame such as their most ambitious
fancies cannot have pictured. Count Inouye, who
holds the portfolio of finance at the time when
these pages are written, remembers how, one win-

ter's night thirty-five years ago, he and a little band of "patriots" applied the torch to the new buildings destined for the British Legation in Tokyo and burned them to the ground. Marquis Ito can recall how he, with the same Count Inouye, made the journey to England as sailors before the mast in 1862, and arrived in London with barely sufficient money to buy a loaf of bread. Marquis Saigo has not forgotten the fight he and his comrades waged thirty-six years ago in the upper story of an inn, when they had to choose between death and abandonment of their anti-foreign crusade. Baron Morioka, who died recently after having occupied many important public posts, was one of two *Samurai* who slashed at three foreigners on the Tokaido in 1862, killing one and wounding the others, which event led to the bombardment of Kagoshima by a British squadron the following year.

Such records are numberless. Nothing is stranger in the story of new Japan than to compare the period of "blood and iron" when these warrior statesmen made their *début* with the era of peaceful progress they have introduced. Mar-

quis Ito will probably leave the most enduring
fame. He is at once the statesman and the
legislator of his time. To him the country owes
its first constitution, promulgated in 1890 and
proudly pointed to by the Japanese nation as the
only charter of the kind voluntarily given by
a sovereign to his subjects. In other countries
such concessions have always been the outcome
of long struggles between ruler and ruled; in
Japan the Emperor freely divested himself of a
portion of his prerogatives and transferred them
to the people. That view of the case is, of course,
not untinged with romance, as will be seen from
what has been written above about the growth
of political parties, but on the whole its truth
cannot be questioned. Marquis Ito and the juris-
consults who helped him to frame the constitution did not err on the side of rashness. They
fixed the minimum age for franchise-holders and
parliamentary candidates at twenty-five and the
property qualification for each alike at payment
of fifteen *yen* annually in the form of direct taxes,
which meant an income of some twelve hundred
yen. The result of the tax-paying limit was

...ly have the most enduring
... the statesmen and the
... to him the country owes
... promulgated in 1890 and
... Japanese nation as the
... voluntarily given by
... In other countries
... has been the outcome
... order and relied; in
... divested himself of a
... and transferred them
... the case is, of course,
... as will be seen from
... more about the growth
... But on the whole its truth
... Marquis Ito and the juris-
... him to frame the constitu-
... on the side of rashness. They
... for franchise-holders and
... candidates at twenty-five and the
... qualification for each able at payment
... annually in the form of direct taxes,
... an income of some twelve hundred
... result of the tax-paying limit was

SANMAI BASHI TEA HOUSE.

that only four hundred and sixty thousand persons were qualified to elect and be elected out of a population numbering sixteen million males of the required age. A bicameral system was adopted for the national assembly: the House of Representatives, numbering three hundred members; the House of Peers, partly hereditary, partly elective and partly nominated by the sovereign. No incident in Japan's modern career was watched with more curiosity than this sudden plunge into parliamentary institutions. There had, indeed, been some preparation. Provincial assemblies — which, as part of the systems of local autonomy gradually introduced after the fall of feudalism, were themselves an innovation — had familiarised the people more or less with the methods of legislative bodies. But provincial assemblies were at best petty arenas — places where the making or mending of roads and the policing and scavenging of villages came up for discussion, and where political parties found no opportunity to attack the government or to debate problems of national interest. Besides, not much was known about provincial assemblies. Only the

briefest outlines of their proceedings appeared in
print; their legislative doings had no general interest, and a vague impression prevailed that if
they were not noticed it was because they did
not deserve attention.   Thus the convening of
a Diet and the sudden transfer of financial and
legislative authority from the throne and an oligarchy of tried statesmen grouped around it to
the hands of men whose qualifications for public
life rested on the verdict of electors themselves
apparently devoid of all light to guide their choice
— this sweeping innovation seemed likely to tax
severely, if not to overtax completely, the progressive capacities of the nation.   What enhanced the
interest of the situation was that the oligarchs
who held the administrative power had taken no
pains to win a following in the political field.
Knowing that the opening of the Diet would be
a veritable letting loose of the dogs of war, an
unmuzzling of the agitators whose mouths had
hitherto been closed by legal restrictions upon
free speech, but who would now enjoy complete
immunity, whatever the nature of their utterances, within the walls of the assembly —

foreseeing all this, the statesmen of the day nevertheless stood severely aloof from alliances of all
kinds, and discharged their administrative functions with apparent indifference to the changes
that popular representation could not fail to induce. That somewhat inexplicable display of
unconcern became partially intelligible when the
constitution was promulgated, for it then appeared
that the cabinet's tenure of office was to depend
solely on the Emperor's will; that ministers were
to take their mandate from the throne, not from
parliament. Here was a fresh illustration of the
theory underlying every part of the Japanese
polity. Laws might be redrafted, institutions remodelled, systems recast, but amid all changes
and mutations one steady point must be carefully preserved, the throne. The makers of new
Japan understood that so long as the sanctity
and inviolability of the Imperial prerogatives
could be preserved, the nation would be held by
a strong anchor from drifting into dangerous
waters. They laboured under no misapprehen-
sion about the inevitable issue of their work in
framing the constitution. They knew very well

that party cabinets are an essential outcome of
representative institutions, and that to party
cabinets Japan must come. But they regarded
the Imperial mandate as a conservative safeguard
pending the organisation and education of parties
competent to form cabinets. Such parties did
not yet exist, and, until they came into unequiv-
ocal existence, the Restoration statesmen, who
had so successfully managed the affairs of the
nation during a quarter of a century, resolved
that the steady point furnished by the throne
must not be abandoned.

On the other hand the agitators found here
a new platform. They had obtained a constitution and a Diet, but they had not obtained an
instrument for pulling down the "clan" administrators, since these stood secure from attack
under the ægis of the sovereign's mandate. They
dared not raise their voices against the unfettered
exercise of the Mikado's prerogative. The
nation, loyal to the core, would not have suffered
such procedure, nor could the agitators themselves have found heart to adopt it. But they
could read their own interpretation into the text

of the constitution, and they could demonstrate practically that a cabinet not acknowledging responsibility to the legislature was virtually impotent for lawmaking purposes.

These are the broad outlines of the contest that began in the first session of the Diet and has continued ever since. The struggle presented varying aspects at different times, but the fundamental question at issue has never changed. Obstruction was the weapon of the political parties. They sought to render legislation and finance impossible for any ministry that refused to take its mandate from the majority in the Lower House, and they imparted an air of respectability and even patriotism ·to their destructive campaign by making " anti-clannism " their war cry, and industriously fostering the idea that the struggle lay between administration guided by public opinion and administration controlled by a clique of clansmen — Satsuma and Choshiu — who stood between the throne and the nation. There could be no doubt about the ultimate success of such tactics. At first the government showed a very resolute front. For five years it ignored the hostility of the Lower House and held by the constitutional principle of responsibility to the Emperor only. In vain the opposition threw out the budget, passed votes of want of confidence, or submitted to the throne addresses impeaching the ministry. The cabinet remained looking calmly down from its high place on the sea of tumult raging below.

It must be confessed that there was something at once sad and impressive in the spectacle. The Restoration statesmen were the men who had made modern Japan; the men who had raised her, in the face of immense obstacles, from the position of an insignificant Oriental state to that of a formidable unit in the comity of nations; the men, finally, who had given to her a constitution and representative institutions. Yet these same men were now fiercely attacked by the arms that they had themselves nerved; were held up to public obloquy as self-seeking usurpers, and were declared to be impeding the people's constitutional route to administrative privileges, when in reality they were only holding the breach until the people should be able to march into the citadel with some show of orderly and competent organisation. That there was no corruption, no abuse of position, is not to be pretended; but, on the whole, the conservatism of the clan statesmen had only one object, to provide that the newly constructed representative machine should not be set working until its parts were duly adjusted and brought into proper gear. There is no doubt that the leaders on both sides understood the situation accurately. The heads of the parties, while they publicly clamoured for parliamentary cabinets, privately confessed that they were not yet prepared to assume administrative responsibilities; and the so-called "clan statesmen," while they refused before the world to accept the Diet's mandates, admitted within official circles that the question was one of time only. It is well to note this mutual understanding, for its existence indicates that the contest must be peaceful throughout.

Little by little, too, the so-called "clan statesmen" are stepping out of the shadow of the throne and associating themselves with the political parties. When that process has been carried somewhat further, party cabinets, with all their drawbacks and disadvantages, will become an accomplished fact, and Japan will have worked her way tranquilly to a goal which other nations reached through scenes of turmoil and even violence.

The expression "tranquilly" is strictly justified by facts. It would have been reasonable to expect that tumult and intemperance must disfigure the proceedings of a Diet whose members were entirely without parliamentary experience, but not without grievances to ventilate, wrongs, real or fancied, to avenge, and abuses to redress. On the whole, however, there has been a remarkable absence of anything like disgraceful license. The politeness, the good temper and the sense of dignity which characterised the Japanese have always saved the situation when it threatened to degenerate into a "scene." Foreigners entering the House of Representatives in Tokyo for the first time might easily misinterpret some of its habits. A number distinguishes each member. It is painted in white on a wooden indicator, the latter being fastened by

F.   :: ::::L.

A FAIR STUDENT.

a hinge to the face of the member's desk.
When present he sets the indicator standing up-
right, and lowers it when leaving the House.
Permission to speak is not obtained by catching
the president's eye, but by calling out the aspir-
ant's number, and as members often emphasise
their calls by hammering their desks with the
indicators, there are moments of decided din.
But for the rest, orderliness and decorum habit-
ually prevail. Speeches have to be made from
a rostrum. There are few displays of oratory or
eloquence. The Japanese formulates his views
with remarkable facility. He is absolutely free
from gaucherie or self-consciousness. He can
think on his feet. But his mind has never
busied itself much with abstract ideas and
subtleties of philosophical or religious thought.
Flights of fancy, impassioned bursts of sentiment, appeals to the heart rather than to the
reason of an audience, are devices strange to
his moral habit. He can be rhetorical, but not
eloquent. In all the parliamentary speeches
hitherto achieved it would be difficult to find a
passage deserving the latter epithet. From the

very outset the debates have been recorded verbatim. Without any forethought of parliamentary reporting, years, indeed, before the date fixed for the promulgation of the constitution, a little band of students elaborated a system of stenography, based on English models, and adapted it to the syllabary of the Japanese language. Their labours remained almost entirely without recognition or remuneration until the Diet met, when it was happily and unexpectedly discovered that a thoroughly competent staff of shorthand reporters could be organised at an hour's notice. Japan can thus boast that, alone among the countries of the world, she possesses an exact record of the proceedings of her Diet from the moment when the first word was spoken within its wall.

We may here remark that the influence of parliamentary debate upon the growth and structure of the Japanese language has been second only to the influence of the newspaper. Chiefly upon the editor and the politician has devolved the duty of presenting to the people in intelligible form the encyclopædia of new conceptions that came in the train of Western civilisation. It is difficult to picture to one's self the dimensions of the task, or to believe that any language could be sufficiently elastic to furnish equivalents for such an endless terminology of absolutely novel philosophies, sciences and systems as the Occident had to offer. But the Japanese language, or, to be more accurate, the Chinese — for the reader will understand that although the pronunciation of words and the construction of sentences differ in Japan and China, the whole vocabulary of the latter country is used in the former — the Japanese language possesses extraordinary potentialities. The easiest way for an Anglo-Saxon to grasp the facts of the case is to suppose that every syllable — not every word but every syllable — of the English language had a distinct meaning of its own, and that the syllables were capable of being combined in groups of two, three, four or five to form new words. It is evident that words thus constructed might be made to express the finest shades of meaning, and that their number would be practically limitless. The

Chinese ideographs are precisely such syllables. There are some twenty thousand of them immediately accessible, and by welding them together in groups of few or many, modern Japanese scholars have filled a lexicon with words which had no existence fifty years ago and would have possessed no meaning for the men of that time, but which accurately convey the sense of the foreign terms they represent. Scarcely a day passes without some addition being made to this lexicon, and the middle and upper ranks of society are becoming more and more permeated with men whose carefully constructed phrases and classical terminology smack of the journalistic article or the parliamentary debate. It is said that when the members of the first Diet read the verbatim report of their first day's proceedings in the *Official Gazette* on the following morning, they were horrified to find all their provincialisms and faults of diction mercilessly reproduced. The quality of their speech has greatly changed since then. Whether the language will undergo that much-discussed radical alteration from an ideographic to an

[116]

alphabetical script is a question which some hesitate to answer and others answer in the negative, but the writer of these pages entertains no doubt whatever on the subject. Nothing marks the stages of a nation's civilisation more emphatically than the nature of the vehicle it employs for transmitting ideas. The stenographist is as far removed from the hieroglyphist as the president of an American college from a Polynesian chief. It is impossible to believe that a people so essentially progressive as the Japanese will permanently condemn themselves to the use of script which renders their literature a sealed book to the whole world of the West and doubles the educational difficulties that their children have to overcome. From his tender years the mind of a Japanese youth is reduced to a mere memorising machine before he has succeeded in engraving upon its tablets the seven or eight thousand ideographs which constitute the equipment of an educated man. If that great, morally injurious and comparatively useless task did not, as it certainly does, handicap him fatally in the race for general knowledge, there would still be the other objection that a nation whose written language is mechanically unintelligible to foreign peoples must always remain isolated. The anti-foreign edicts of the early Tokugawa *Shoguns* have been torn up; the "barbarian-expelling" fanaticism of mediæval times has been replaced by a frank though self-asserting liberalism; the essentials of Occidental civilisation have entered in to dwell side by side with the refinements and artistic etiquette of old Japan; but all the thoughts of the people in this era of wonderful progress, all the impressions that they receive from contact with the systems and sciences of Europe and America, are either completely hidden from the eyes of the nations whose intimacy they court, or find halting expression in the clumsy renderings of incompetent translators. Can such a state of affairs be permanent? The truth is that the Japanese have not yet awakened fully to the importance of this problem. The sense of proportion, which owes so much of its development to opportunities for observation, is necessarily defective among them.

The conventionalisms of classic Chinese they understand and appreciate, but when they enter the field of general diction, they seem unable to estimate how much the force of an idea owes to the form of its expression. An industrious purveyor sits proudly under a signboard informing the public that he sells "extract of fowl" (*i. e.*, eggs); a haberdasher with a large foreign *clientèle* sports the legend "Ladies furnished in the upper story;" a blacksmith blows his bellows behind an announcement that he has been "imstracted by French horse-leach;" the editors of a magazine for teaching English make a lady "puff at her tiny pipe in order to dissemble herself," or a startled father "roar out, taking it for a mischief of some naughty boy;" and the educational authorities go to the highways and byways to pick up "professors" of European tongues. Thus the nation is content to imagine that its mental processes and the trend of its intelligence are adequately depicted through the agency of a host of hybrid publications the outgrowth of recent enterprise, newspapers, brochures and magazines, their pages

inscribed with ideas which, if they do not ema-
nate from the vapoury and immature fancies of
callow students, are robbed of all dignity and
grace by the grotesqueness of the language employed to express them. Just as the nation fails
to detect how greatly its intelligence is misrep-
resented by such media, so its perception has not
been aroused to the barbarous clumsiness of the
ideographs and to the impenetrable barrier they
oppose to free interchange of thought. But that
an effective sense of these disadvantages will
be born sooner or later, no observer of Japan's
progress can doubt.

Materials for constructing a language adapted to
parliamentary requirements, or, indeed, to the requirements of any science or philosophy, are thus
abundant in Japan, but the method of procedure
in the Diet is not calculated to encourage oratori-
cal displays. Every measure of importance has to
be submitted to a committee, and not until the
latter's report has been received does serious debate
take place. But in ninety-nine cases out of every
hundred the committee's report determines the
attitude of the house, and speeches are felt to be

JAPAN

... even ... which, if they do ... ...
... the ... and familiar tastes of
... states ... tables, of all dignity and
... by ... ... of the language em-
... ... Just as the nation fills
... greatly its intelligence is misrep-
... ... so its perception has not
... ... the barren closeness of the
... and ... happ... the border they
... to free ... of thought. But that
... ... of these disadvantages will
... ... it, no observer of Japan's
... ...

... ... contorting a language adapted to
... any requirements, or, indeed, to the re-
... ... or philosophy, are they
... in ... a. but the method of procedure
... the ... is calculated to encourage oratori-
cal displays. Every measure of importance has to
be submitted to a committee, and until the
... report has been received no serious debate
... place. But in ninety-nine cases out of every
hundred the committee's report determines the
... ... of the house, and speeches are wasted

[221]

TEACHING YOUNG GIRLS TO WRITE.

more or less superfluous. One result of this system is that business is done with a degree of
celerity scarcely known in Occidental legislatures.
For example, the meetings of the House of Representatives during the session 1896–97 were thirty-
two, and the number of hours occupied by the
sittings aggregated a hundred and sixteen. Yet
the result was fifty-five bills debated and passed,
several of them measures of prime importance, as
the gold-standard bill, the budget, a statutory tariff
bill, and so on. Such a record seems difficult to
reconcile with any idea of careful legislation; but
it must be remembered that although actual sittings of the Houses are comparatively few and
brief, the committees remain constantly at work
from morning to evening throughout the nine
weeks of the session's duration. Another interesting feature of the system is that the members of
the government do not lead their supporters in the
Diet or break lances with their opponents. The
ministers of State and the delegates from each
administrative department are entitled to be
present and to address the Houses whenever they
please. They avail themselves of the privilege to

the extent of explaining official bills or answering questions. But they never take any part in a debate or make controversial speeches. It is a somewhat lame system; for while it brings the members of the cabinet and the government's delegates within range of the opposition's invective, it does not enable them to exert any sensible influence on a debate. Nevertheless there is no gainsaying the fact that the legislative laurels have been won entirely by the government, session after session. Thus, in the 1896–97 session alluded to above, out of fifty-five measures debated and passed only three were private bills — a strong corroboration of the criticism that whatever destructive capacity has hitherto been displayed by Japanese political parties, their competence for purposes of constructive statesmanship remains an entirely undemonstrated quality.

That the aspiration common to political parties the world over, namely, parliamentary cabinets, would find expression in Japan also, might have been foretold by any student of constitutional history. But we have to answer the more complicated and interesting question, what is the ultimate tendency of political thought in Japan, and what will be the final lines of party cleavage? It must be confessed at once that these points are still wrapped in much obscurity. With the records of eleven sessions of the Diet and the platform utterances of many years to guide us, there should not be any insuperable difficulty in drawing definite inferences. Yet, when we proceed to catalogue the objects for which politicians have hitherto fought, we find that the list does not include anything particularly suggestive. Reduction of the land tax, freedom of speech and pen, party cabinets, petty modifications of the local-government system, abuses of official power, acts of financial dishonesty, administrative reform, treaty revision and foreign affairs, — such are the matters that have chiefly occupied political attention. In view of what has already been written about taxation in general and the land tax in particular, it may seem strange that a reduction of the agricultural classes' burdens should have been gravely advocated by any association of politicians. But in the early days of Japan's parliamentary career the people's representatives, posing for the first time in that character, were naturally anxious to play the part of popular benefactors. Lighter taxes were the most obvious means to that end, and as from time immemorial the nation's contributions to the administration had been virtually limited to the land tax, the latter suggested itself as the proper object of attack, quite apart from fiscal justice or expediency. An incident so commonplace would scarcely be worth special mention had it not led to curious complications. In order to cut down the land tax some other source of revenue had to be found, or some retrenchment of expenditures had to be effected. The latter method was chosen, and, as a matter of course, the reformers concluded that the proper domain to be invaded was that of official salaries. Now the number of officials engaged in administering Japan's affairs is forty-two thousand seven hundred and twenty-eight, and their yearly stipends total thirteen million six hundred and sixty-eight thousand two hundred and forty-six *yen*, so that their average monthly pay is less than eleven dollars (gold). There does not seem to be much room for retrenchment there, and the case presents itself in a still more striking light when we note that the one thousand six hundred and seventy-four judges and public procurators who constitute the judiciary receive an average salary of thirty-six and one half dollars (gold) a month, and that the seventy-three thousand one hundred and sixty teachers engaged in the primary schools have to make ends meet with a monthly pittance of a little over three and one half dollars. It is plain that official integrity and competence cannot possibly be looked for under such circumstances. When a common factory hand can earn more than a school teacher, and when a clerk in a store gets as much as a judge on the bench, the judicial and educational careers will never attract men of talent. In fact, Japan's present attitude is one of financial shrinking from the responsibilities of her new career. She is like a youth who engages in every kind of exercise calculated to promote his growth, yet seeks all the while to clothe himself in the garments of his boyhood. Her administrators are not free from peculation, her judiciary from corruption, her officials from incompetence; nor will they ever be free until the emoluments of office become more important than its opportunities. Blind to that rudimentary truth, the opposition in the first House of Representatives — and practically the whole House was in opposition — made a fierce onset upon official salaries. They had no right to meddle with the matter: the constitution explicitly reserves to the sovereign the prerogative of appointing and dismissing officials and fixing their stipends. But the House, as we have said, was in a destructive mood. If it might not constitutionally legislate for a reduction of salaries, it could at any rate refuse to pass any budget including payments on the old scale. That was what it did. Probably these party politicians had no immediate object beyond providing means to reduce the land tax. But they incidentally achieved another result: they placed the so-called "clan statesmen" in the doubly invidious position of clinging to power in the interest of the clans as opposed to the interest of the nation at large, and of refusing to abate anything of their own emoluments for the sake of lightening the burdens of the people. It says much for the resolution and foresight of those statesmen that they stood firm under such circumstances. The event has justified them, for to-day the nation recognises that a programme precisely the converse of that advocated by the people's representatives seven years ago must be adopted, the land tax must be increased and official salaries must be augmented. This chapter of parliamentary history indicates that political wisdom is still monopolised by the men whom the tumult of the revolution brought to the surface thirty years ago, and who have remained on the surface ever since. With them victory has rested from point to point of the struggle against the party politicians. Administrative reform, for example, has always been a principal plank in the platform of every political party, but no party has ever yet clearly explained its conception of reform, and the *Meiji* statesmen, by quietly waiting for an explanation, have seen the agitation perish from anæmia of ideas. Similarly in the case of treaty revision the party leaders would have pushed the government out of the broad path of patient and conciliatory effort into a narrow groove of retaliation and reprisal. But the government never wavered, and the goal was ultimately reached without any sacrifice of national dignity or loss of foreign friendship. In short, Japan's best hope of attaining the international position whither her gaze is directed seems to centre upon the band of statesmen who still enjoy the confidence of the sovereign, and upon the younger officials who, educated under their instruction, are now gradually stepping into their places. The reader will easily understand, therefore, how essential it is to the political parties that they should succeed in enrolling these *Meiji* statesmen in their ranks. There have been indications that such success was on the point of achievement. In 1895, Marquis Ito, then Prime Minister, stepped out of the shadow of the throne and formed a coalition with the Liberal party. The proximate purpose of the union was to secure the Diet's assent to a large programme of measures — including naval and military expansion — mapped out by the cabinet in the sequel of the war with China. But it is certain that Marquis Ito, the framer of the constitution, the leading statesman of Japan, the Emperor's most trusted minister, did not for a moment mistake the significance of his own act. He knew exactly what

A GROUP OF JAPANESE NOBLES AND DIGNITARIES.

was involved in an open alliance between the cabinet and a political party; knew that it must be interpreted by the nation as a confession of the cabinet's inability to conduct State affairs without the aid of a majority in the Lower House; knew that it indicated an advance almost to the very threshold of the English system of parliamentary mandate and Imperial indorsement; and knew that his association with the Liberals supplied the lack which had hitherto incapacitated them as serious candidates for office, the lack of administrative experience and prestige. It seemed now that the struggle had virtually come to an end, and that the principle of party cabinets had received practical recognition. But less than three years afterwards the same Marquis Ito found himself at the head of a cabinet with the same Liberals in opposition. His predecessor in the premiership, Count Matsukata, had assumed office with the support of the Progressists, and had resigned it with the same Progressists in opposition.

What is the explanation of these things? Simply this, that on the one hand the political parties have been so long trained in habits of irresponsible criticism as to be temporarily unfit for the duties of responsible alliance, and that, on the other, since their allegiance is to persons, not principles, they are without any strong force of cohesion or working sense of discipline. By what processes of education they are to be fitted for the *rôle* they aspire to fill, it is impossible to predict, but in the working out of every Japanese problem allowance must always be made for those factors of versatility and adaptiveness which have hitherto helped the nation so signally through all its difficulties. Some students of the time predict that the issue will be a falling asunder of the two great clans, Satsuma and Choshiu, and that their rupture will mark the line of division in the new political field; the Satsuma men, on one side, standing independent of political parties and ruling it may be by military force; the Choshiu men ranged on the other, leading the political parties and fighting for parliamentary cabinets. To the writer such a forecast seems superficial. The Satsuma men are richly endowed with the opportunist faculty. Their position in this final act of the Restoration drama finds an exact analogy in the part they played at the rising of the curtain thirty-five years ago. When the national mind was beginning to seethe with the idea of abolishing military feudalism and restoring the administrative power to the sovereign as a preliminary step to representative institutions, and when the Choshiu men stood forth as champions of the great change, the Satsuma clan joined hands with the Aizu to crush the movement and to drive its supporters from the capital; but when the tendency of the era could no longer be mistaken, Satsuma turned and combined with Choshiu to annihilate Aizu. Proceedings of that kind were perfectly consistent with the historical character of the southern clan. Its leaders are not quick to read the signs of the times, but they are conspicuously quick to obey the legend when the writing has become clear. If at one moment (1897) in the *Meiji* era circumstances forced them away from their old allies and, by separating them from the two great political parties, placed them in the false position of opposing parliamentary cabinets, there was no difficulty in foreseeing that the expediency of advocating parliamentary cabinets would presently draw them

[131]

back to the alliance, as, indeed, the event proved. Is it, then, in the field of foreign politics that the dividing lines of public opinion are likely to be finally traced? At first sight an affirmative answer suggests itself, for during the past six years a very distinct differentiation between "stalwarts" and "moderates" has been apparent. But here, too, a bewildering feature disturbs our calculations. The so-called "stalwarts" show a marked disposition to condemn the extensive programme of armament expansion which the "moderates" uncompromisingly support. So, in fine, we rise from every examination of Japanese politics with a conviction that if the tests employed for analytical purposes in Western countries are applicable here, the non-official section of the people has not learned how to adapt its methods to its fancies, or acquired any sober idea of the responsibilities attaching to the control of national affairs. After all, the solid ballast that keeps the foreign policy of every Western state on an even keel is self-interest. Moral principles are regarded as mere deck cargo, to be thrown overboard without compunction in rough waters. The Japanese have not risen fully to that elevated canon of international practice. They still cherish a romantic idea that a nation, like an individual, should endeavour to tread the "*Samurai's* road," the *bushi-do* of feudal days, on which the four conspicuous finger-posts are loyalty, truth, magnanimity and courage. Though not generally credited it is nevertheless true that ninety-nine out of every hundred Japanese frankly regarded the recent war with China as a chivalrous effort on their country's part to secure the independence of little weak Korea against the present menace of big strong China's grasp and the ominous shadow of future Russian aggression. Side by side with that conviction was a passionate longing to win the credit of rousing both China and Korea from their blind conservatism, and thus obtaining for Japan world-wide recognition as the propagator of Occidental civilisation in the Orient.

XXIII

RECENT PROGRESS

By K. Asakawa, Ph.D., *Dartmouth College*

NE MAY NATURALLY SUP- pose that the most remarkable progress of recent events in Japan must be found in the evolution of her foreign relations which have culminated in the great war now waging between her and Russia. Some of the deeper causes, however, of the activity, both at home and abroad, of the Japanese people may be sought in the peculiar conditions of their economic life. It is safe to say that it is these profound material forces which have powerfully impelled the people to seek, even by means of destructive warfare, a solution of their national problem, and which will continue to suggest, in a large measure, the course of their domestic and international conduct. We shall, therefore, devote this

chapter to the consideration of some of the
fundamental points of the material progress
of Japan in recent years.

The first feature of the economic life of Japan
may be said to consist in the relatively decreas-
ing importance of her agriculture on the one
hand and the rapidly increasing importance
of her manufacture and trade on the other, or,
in other words, in the fact that Japan is fast
passing from an agricultural to an industrial
stage of her economic development. The tendency
is at once indicated, as in all industrial countries,
in the slow growth of the rural population
in comparison with the urban. If all towns
containing each over ten thousand inhabitants
are considered as urban communities and all
the smaller towns as rural, it is seen that the
population of the former increases five or six
per cent yearly, while the corresponding rate
with the latter never rises above three per cent
and is usually much lower. The reasons for
this phenomenon are many and important. As
is well known, Japan is richly endowed with a
sedimentary soil which is well suited for the

culture of cereals, and which in some localities yields two, three and even four different crops during the year, but these advantages are seriously counterbalanced by the limited extent of the arable land of the country. The area actually under cultivation cannot be more than thirteen million acres, that is, less than fourteen per cent of the total area of Japan proper. On the other hand, owing to the hilly nature of the country, the reclaimable area must be relatively small. It is evident, therefore, that the future increase of Japan's agricultural resources must be sought less by extensive cultivation than by intensive improvement. But here again the outlook is not reassuring. The Japanese farmer expends the minutest care in the cultivation of his precious land, and the scientific progress of the twentieth century is not likely to render his methods much more intensive or to greatly increase the productivity of his soil. The most impressive illustration, however, of Japan's limited agricultural resources is the rate which her arable area bears to her population. The ratio — either of the arable land to the entire

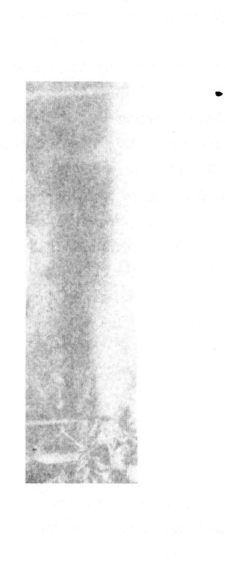

... ... which in some localities
... ... and even four different crops
... ... but these advantages are
... ... by the limited extent
... ... of the country. The area
... ... under cultivation cannot be more than
... ... million acres, that is, less than fourteen
per cent of the total area of Japan proper. On
the other hand, owing to the hilly nature of the
country, the ... tenable area must be relatively
small. It is evident, therefore, that the future
increase of Japan's agricultural resources must
be sought less by extensive cultivation than
by intensive improvement. But here again the
outlook is not reassuring. The Japanese farmer
expends the minutest care in the cultivation
of his precious land, and the scientific progress
of the twentieth century is not likely to render
his methods much more intensive or to greatly
increase the productivity of his soil. The most
impressive illustration, however, of Japan's
... agricultural resources is the rate which
... arable area bears to her population. The
... ... of the arable land to the entire

KAGO BEARERS.

population or of the cultivated land to the farming population — is less than half an acre per head. From this it naturally follows that the cultivated lots are diminutive, more than a half of the rice fields of the country being each less than one eighth of an acre. Under these circumstances, the life of the Japanese farmer is anything but enviable. He is obliged to exercise the utmost care in utilising every scrap of his land and every grain of his yield. The farm-labourers are content with low wages, seldom rising above thirty-five cents per day for the male and twenty cents for the female, while the proprietor bears the burden of high rates of interest as well as of national and local taxes. The life of the farmer would have been utterly abject had it not been for the following two fortunate circumstances: namely, that in Japan great landowners are comparatively few and most tenants are themselves owners of petty lots; and that the silk, tea or cotton culture affords a subsidiary occupation to the farming family whose income would otherwise be too meagre for subsistence. Thanks to these con-

ditions, the hard life of the Japanese farmer has
not been able to dim his naturally cheerful disposition. Japan, however, cannot help realising
that her agriculture is already failing either to
supply her growing manufacture with sufficient
raw material or to feed and support the new
population which is increasing annually at the
rate of over half a million.

Had agriculture been the only means of
Japan's sustenance, her future as a nation would
have been sealed. The difference, however, between the stationary condition of her agriculture
and the rapid growth of her manufacture and
trade becomes every year more distinct and
decisive. Until one comprehends this significant
difference, he fails to realise one of the most
fundamental causes which move Japan onward
with an irresistible force into a commanding
position in the far East. Let us briefly consider
the manner in which Japan has entered upon an
industrial career. Before she was thrown open
to the world's trade, there had existed in Japan
highly developed manual industries, but she had
been entirely unacquainted with the operations

of modern machineries. Under these circumstances, it is not strange that, as soon as she began her commercial intercourse with the Western nations, she found herself confronted by an economic situation to which she was unable to adjust herself. The keen sense of novelty excited among the people by the sudden inflow of new goods into the market resulted in a wonderfully fast growth of the consumption of these articles. The existing five per cent. import duty, which peculiar circumstances had rendered almost equal to no duty, further stimulated the impetuous advance of imports over exports. The old manual industries were largely upset by the revolution of consumption, while the latter progressed so swiftly that the new industries, for the upbuilding of which the nation lacked the necessary skill and capital, found it impossible to overtake it. The outcome was a state of almost complete economic dependence of the nation upon foreign production. It was here that the energy of the nation and the sagacity of the government were again brought to a severe test. The disadvantageous tariff having years

[139]

before been imposed upon the feeble Yedo administration, and having since been mercilessly enforced by the foreigners against the nation, to the latter's manifest loss and deep resentment, the Japanese Government entered upon a long series of attempts to revise the foreign treaties and thereby, among other things, to regain the lost tariff autonomy of the nation. The revision was at last effected in 1894, and the new treaties which emancipated Japan from the consular jurisdiction of the foreign residents and gave her a partial tariff autonomy came into force in 1899. At the same time that the efforts for this revision were begun, the government also endeavoured to encourage the more important new industries by means of subsidies and examples. It is beyond a doubt that in this process blunders and abuses arose between the members of the government and the inexperienced business men, but it largely goes to the credit of the latter that, as soon as the authorities were thus compelled to aid the new movement, industry and trade began to grow side by side and with increasing speed. The tremendous expansion of

Japan's economic resources thus inaugurated has been such that, not only the home consumption is now adequately met by the home production — not only the domestic market has well-nigh reached its "saturation point," but the commerce is already rapidly expanding *abroad*. The foreign trade, which amounted to only forty million *yen* in 1871, promises in 1904 to reach six hundred and fifty millions — a growth of 1,625 per cent within thirty-four years. That this truly phenomenal progress of foreign trade has been due to the corresponding expansion of manufacture will be presently discussed, but the fact will be apparent even now when it is seen that the exportation of manufactured articles increased from ten million *yen* in 1890, to seventy-four million and seven hundred thousand in 1900, and further to more than two hundred and forty millions in 1908. Simultaneously with this increase of the exportation of manufactured goods, the import trade has shown more rapid growth in the items of raw articles and machineries than in those of foreign manufactures, and the significance of this tendency is patent.

JAPAN

If, as has been said, Japan's future greatness lies in an industrial career, it is important to know how well qualified she is as a manufacturing nation. Certain grave disadvantages at once suggest themselves which are seriously hampering the industrial progress of Japan, — namely, her want of new labour and business experience and of certain raw materials and capital. As regards labour, her elaborate system of apprenticeship and her manual skill were once the pride of old Japan, but time has radically changed the aspect of her economic organisation. Until the old labour is satisfactorily transformed into an organised and specialised mechanical dexterity, the Japanese mill-hand will inevitably continue to show the inefficiency and ill discipline which still characterise them. Nor will Japan be able forever to rely upon the cheap cost of her labour, for the wages have already risen more than a hundred per cent during the last fifteen years, and will keep rising with the general standard of life. The want of the proper experience of the Japanese manufacturer may well be accounted for by his recent appearance in the business world. He has shown himself to be unduly eager to rid himself of the foreign adviser or middleman, whose service would be valuable in supplying him with a ready knowledge of the conditions of foreign production and foreign market. At the same time, it may be said, the native manufacturer, when he is thrown upon his own resources, will learn deeper by blundering more, than under the guidance of a foreigner. A more serious charge has often been made against the defective commercial veracity of the Japanese, which is admitted by themselves to have been real to some extent, but which has for certain reasons been greatly exaggerated by foreign critics, while it is naturally being remedied by the business experience of which they, unlike their Chinese neighbours, have hitherto been lamentably in need.

As to the lack of the necessary capital, it is not to be wondered at when we recall that Japan is only emerging from an agricultural stage of life, but it none the less embarrasses her economic enterprise at home and abroad to an unendurable extent. The only natural remedy in this respect appears to be either to induce foreigners to invest their surplus capital in Japanese undertakings, or to extend the trade with the neighbouring countries as vigorously as the small capital of Japan will allow and thereby gradually multiply its volume and its usefulness. It is obvious that both methods should be applied side by side. The former method has already been started on a modest scale in oil and tobacco industries and in some municipal undertakings. When certain difficulties of law and business which still stand in the way are, as they will be, amended, the high rates of interest which prevail in the money market of Japan will become a sufficient inducement to an increasing investment of foreign capital. As to the latter method, that is, the realising of larger capital through trade, it has since the war with China been proceeding with considerable success. A tremendous advance of the process would follow a victory over Russia in the present conflict and the consequent "open door" in Manchuria and Korea. The last great drawback upon the progress of Japan's industry is her want of some important raw materials for manufacture, particularly cotton, wool, and iron. Cotton has to be imported every year from India and China to the value of nearly

A CURBSTONE MERCHANT.

sixty million *yen*. Wool has to be entirely supplied from abroad, as pastures for sheep are practically non-existent in Japan, while her total annual output of iron is less than eighty thousand tons.

Fortunately for Japan, the disadvantages above enumerated which impede her industrial advance are in their nature neither permanent nor irremediable. Her labour and experience cannot help gaining by time, while her internal and external progress will enable her to acquire foreign capital and raw material in larger quantities and with greater ease. Over against these diminishing disadvantages, Japan commands an unrivalled geographical position between the great Pacific Ocean on the one hand and the teeming millions of the East Asiatic nations on the other, the commercial importance of both of which must grow wonderfully with the development of canals and railways in various parts of the world and the opening of new markets in the yet slightly explored East. This superb Phenicia-like situation of Japan toward the outside world is supplemented internally by a richly endowed soil and an eager and ambitious race.

JAPAN

It is well known that the soil of Japan possesses an abundant water supply and extensive coal beds, the latter already yielding nearly ten million tons per annum, and produces tea and silk, the peculiar qualities of which are hardly to be imitated by the products of other lands. The ambition and docility of the people would appear to be well exemplified by the phenomenal growth of the silk and cotton textile industries, which have risen twenty-fold in value during the last two decades, and by the creation of certain new, prosperous industries, particularly in matting, lucifer matches, straw braids, and cotton yarns. The exportation of the six principal branches of manufactures here enumerated amounted in 1888 to only less than thirty-one million *yen*, but in 1908 to one hundred and seventy-eight millions. It should be remembered also that none of these articles have found their way into the foreign market without encountering embarrassing difficulties at home and a sharp competition abroad, and that with a remission of effort they would at once sink into insignificance.

Considering Japan's foreign trade apart from

her manufacture, it is gratifying to see that its development during the past decade has been rapid and also on the whole regular. The exports in 1903 amounted, for instance, to 289.5 million *yen*, which meant a gain of 222.7 per cent over those of 1893, and the imports, to 317.1 millions, or a gain of 259.3 per cent, while the total volume of trade showed 606.6 millions, that is, nearly three and a half times as large as it was ten years before. Let us now analyse these trade figures, in order to discover some of the most significant tendencies of Japan's trade and of her national growth in general, — for we maintain that it is impossible to comprehend the meaning of many of the recent events in the progress of Japan without a knowledge of her economic life. Taking first the import figures, which have risen from twenty-eight million *yen* in 1878 to more than three hundred and seventeen millions in 1903, we note that the growth is mainly due to causes which may be classified as follows: firstly, the progress of industries, resulting in an increasing demand, on the one hand, for machineries, and, on the other, for raw materials, particularly cotton and iron; secondly, a great advance of the standard of living among the people at large, which caused a remarkable growth of the general consumption of imported articles, including textiles, woollens, petroleum, small wares of luxury, and various other items; and thirdly, the rapid increase of population, coupled with the transition of the new nation from an agricultural to a manufacturing stage of economics, which, besides aiding the growth of general consumption as stated above, necessitated a remarkable development of the importation of food-stuff, such as rice, beans and peas, flour and sugar. Wearisome as it may seem, it is essential to keep in mind these three classes of causes apart, for they have tended and will continue to induce the import trade to grow, not only with rapidity, but also, as the figures plainly show, in varying degrees from one another. And it is precisely in this difference that one of the striking indications of Japan's call in the East may be discerned. Let us now briefly specify this important differ-

ence.   In the first place, the increase of importation due to the second group of causes,
namely, the growth of the general consumption
of foreign goods, has not been nearly as fast as
that of the other classes of imports, for the
patent reason that Japan is able to supply her
people more and more with the fruits of her
own manufacture, which itself is progressing
rapidly.   While there is no reason why the
future increase of this class of imports — that is,
goods for general consumption — will not be
steady, it at the same time may not be rapid
save in the case of a few exceptional articles.   Nor
may the importation of machineries excepting
the most advanced ones, such as locomotives, be
expected to grow more rapidly, the ground
for this negative supposition being again the
increasing activity of Japan's manufacturing life.
The other two classes of imports, however, that
is to say, the raw materials for manufacture and
the food-stuffs for the growing population, have
shown a tremendous advance, and may safely
be said to command the most assured promise
for the future.   A glance at the following table

will make an elaborate demonstration of our statement superfluous : —

IMPORTATION OF RAW MATERIAL AND FOOD-STUFF (Unit, 1,000,000 *yen*)				
	1882	1892	1902	1903
Cotton	0.46	12.32	79.78	69.52
Pig iron	0.09	0.24	0.98	1.25
Wool	?	0.30	3.40	4.81
Sugar	3.84	9.53	14.36	20.96
Rice.	0.21[1]	1.86[1]	13.56[1]	51.96
Flour	?	0.27	3.28	10.32
Beans	?	?	4.95	6.37
(Oil cakes	0.03	0.82	10.12	10.73)

[1] The average for the past ten years inclusive.

This remarkable showing of figures becomes highly significant when we consider further that — to this point is called the particular attention of the reader — most of the articles the importation of which increases the fastest come mainly from the East Asiatic countries. With the exception of most flour and some iron coming from the United States, which country, as we shall see presently, occupies a unique relation to Japan's trade, we observe that India furnishes the bulk of cotton, while North China and Manchuria send their beans and oil cakes, and Korea is beginning to be a granary of Japan. Thus we come to a conclusion of great moment that Japan is obliged to depend in an increasing measure for her most important articles for importation upon East Asia, to which she is, both geographically and historically, most intimately connected.

An analysis of the export figures of Japan leads us from another direction to a conclusion strikingly similar to the above. We have already emphasised that, as contrary to the trend of her import trade, Japan's exportation consists yearly more of manufactured articles and less of raw goods than before. Here again a deeper significance is disclosed by an examination of the destination of the exports. In spite of the oft-heard cry of an industrial "yellow peril," the time, if ever, seems very remote when Japan may invade Europe and America with her manufacture and compete with the products of their superior machinery and mechanical experience. Her exportation to Western countries already has a clear indication of settling down to two main classes of articles: such unfinished goods as raw silk, copper, sulphur, and others, which might rather be finished there than here, and certain goods peculiar to the soil of Japan, as, for instance, tea, *habutai* and other light silk fabrics, porcelain, matting, camphor, and the like. The exportation of these articles must increase in varying degrees, according to the state of several determining factors that rule the domestic and foreign markets, but its future on the whole is plainly much more limited and inelastic than that of Japan's exports to the East Asiatic countries. To these latter Japan's close trade relation has become all the more manifest since she began to be a manufacturing nation, while they remained agricultural; she buys from them raw products and food-stuffs, and supplies them with her manufactured articles. The demand for these last-named articles, also, by a fortunate coincidence of circumstances, is at present what the still inferior skill of the Japanese manufacturer can supply. The taste of the Eastern buyer is still low and his wants still relatively few, while their advance may be expected to run parallel to Japan's gradual improvement in

WEIGHING TEA.

industries. Her neighbours in Korea, Eastern Siberia, Manchuria, North and South China, India, and Indo-China and the Philippines, absorb her coal, matches, marine products, cotton yarns and coarse cotton fabrics, and other similar goods, already to the amount of 126.7 million *yen* (in 1903), while ten years before they consumed twenty-three millions, and in 1882 only six millions. From these significant data, the conclusion seems tenable that her geographical and economical conditions render it natural for Japan to interpret the new civilisation of the Occident for the old Orient, and create new wants in the latter of the fruits of the former, herself repeating an important share of profits that accrue from the worldwide exchange. This share will consist in an even closer economic connection with Japan than at present prevails of East Asia, particularly Korea and China, as her grand supply region of raw goods and market for made articles. In comparison with this, Japan's trade with countries of Western civilisation may become more and more a mere supplement to her Eastern trade.

To this general statement a unique exception

[153]

must be taken in the case of Japan's trade with the United States. The latter is to-day, as she was twenty years ago, the largest single buyer of Japanese goods, notably tea, raw silk, matting, porcelain and camphor. In the import trade, while the United States is second to Great Britain in the list of Japan's sellers, the former advanced in the twenty years between 1882 and 1902 from 3 to 48.6 million *yen*, and the latter only from 14 to 50.3 millions. The most peculiar feature of the American trade of Japan which is not found in her European commerce is found in the singular fact that the United States buys considerable quantities of crude or unfinished Japanese articles, and sells in return an increasing amount of raw cotton and flour and other food-stuffs, thus participating in a large measure in the peculiarities of the Japanese trade with the East. The United States also furnishes Japan certain products of modern industries more cheaply than Europe, from which she once was wont to purchase those articles. Moreover, the United States is able to export to China and Korea certain manufactured goods which would otherwise be supplied mostly by Japan.

The American trade with the Orient in general seems bound to grow to an unheard-of extent, and a sharp competition might presently ensue between Japan and the United States in this lucrative trade before an adjustment of their respective interests shall have been, as they will naturally be, effected.

We conclude our brief survey of Japan's foreign trade by appending a table showing its distribution by the continents. The table is self-explanatory, and from it one will readily infer that, if Japan would exist and grow as a nation, she must dispute any other Power standing in the way of her all-important Eastern trade, and must demand at all cost an opportunity equal to that enjoyed by other nations for economic enterprise in Korea and China. Japan's material interests in these countries imperatively call for, not an exclusive exploitation of their resources either by herself or by any other nation, but a free competition there within the extent which is open to all other trading nations, — in short, a strict application in Korea and China of the so-called principle of the " open door." Upon the success or failure of this principle will the fate of Japan as a nation depend, for nothing would more certainly bring about her slow decay and sure retrogression than the exclusion from the Asiatic continent of her merchandise for sale and for purchase and of her emigrants. The world of the far East can hardly hold together the open policy upheld by Japan and an exclusive policy, be the latter supported by the great Russian Empire.

DISTRIBUTION OF JAPAN'S FOREIGN TRADE BY CONTINENTS (Unit, 1,000,000 *yen*)				
	EUROPE	AMERICA	EAST ASIA	AUSTRALIA AND OTHERS
1881 { Exports . . .	12.5	11.0	0.6	0.9
1881 { Imports . . .	21.0	1.8	7.6	0.5
1891 { Exports . . .	23.9	31.1	20.9	1.8
1891 { Imports . . .	30.3	6.8	23.7	1.9
1901 { Exports . . .	59.9	75.6	111.4	5.2
1901 { Imports . . .	96.7	42.9	109.0	7.0
1903 { Exports . . .	70.3	85.7	126.7	6.7
1903 { Imports . . .	96.1	46.7	169.1	5.0

XXIV

RECENT PROGRESS

By K. Asakawa, Ph. D., *Dartmouth College*

(Concluded)

URING THE TEN YEARS between the close of the Chinese war of 1894–95 and the outbreak of hostilities with Russia in 1904, Japan's foreign relations underwent a development hardly less rapid, and far more dramatic, than the phenomenal growth of her industry and trade, which has been the subject of our discussion in the foregoing chapter. This remarkable evolution of the diplomatic and political activity abroad of the Japanese nation consisted, in a large measure, in a profound divergence of the interests of Japan and Russia in the far East — a divergence which has unfolded itself with unerring and tragic swiftness, until the

two empires are now found in the midst of the most colossal warfare known in their history. Let us briefly describe in the following pages how history led from one event to another in this memorable decade, and how finally diplomacy gave place to war.

It is hardly necessary to recount the story of the Russian acquisition, in 1858–60, of the vast territory lying between the Ussuri and lower Amur Rivers and the Gulf of Tartary, and of the building, in the latter year, of Vladivostok at the southern extremity of the new province. This expansion of the Russian territory in the East may be considered as only another step in the irresistible southward march of the boundary of the great empire. Vladivostok was ice-bound in winter and was far from being adequate as the naval headquarters of Russia on the Pacific coast, while its unworthiness as the terminus of the Siberian Railway became evident as soon as the construction of the latter was finally decided upon, about 1890. If Russia would grow as a great naval and commercial power in Asia, she should by all means gain possession of an ice-free outlet on the Pacific coast. An opportunity came in April, 1895, when, at the close of her unsuccessful war with Japan, China again appealed to Russia to interfere, showing her the terms of peace which China had been called upon by Japan to accept. One of these terms was the cession to the island empire of the Liao-tung peninsula containing Port Arthur. Russia was as fully alive to the permanent irreparable injury which this stipulation would inflict upon her own interest in the East, as to the equally immense advantage that her own possession of the same territory would give to herself. The reader will still remember how the government of the Czar succeeded in securing the coöperation of France and Germany in their joint coercion of Japan, and how on May 10 the Japanese Emperor issued an edict acknowledging the "friendly" counsel of the three Powers and announcing the complete retrocession of the Liao-tung peninsula to the Chinese Empire. The identical notes of the Powers had stated, as is now well known, that Japan's retention of the territory was considered by them not only as imperilling the Chinese capital, but also as making Korean independence illusory, and, consequently, prejudicial to the permanent peace of the far East. The real meaning of the coercion was, however, well understood alike by the intervening Powers and by Japan; nor shall we fail to observe it when we come to relate what happened three years hence upon the same ground.

Let us pause a moment before we discuss subsequent events, and make an attempt to comprehend the historical significance of this memorable incident of 1895. The present writer has elsewhere [1] expressed his views upon this point in the following manner: —

"It is not too much to say that with this incident Eastern Asiatic history radically changed its character, for it marks the beginning of a new era in which the struggle is waged no longer among the Oriental nations themselves, but between different sets of interests and principles which characterise human progress

---

[1] K. Asakawa, *Russo-Japanese Conflict* (Boston, 1904), pp. 77-82.

CAN

. . . . d by . . .
. C . . . capita . .
. . force theory,
. . the . . . . .
. . . . meaning of . . .
. . . . . understood . .
. . . . . and by Japan . . .
. . it when we . . . . .
. . . . years hence 1901

. . . . . . before we discuss
. . . . make an attempt to
. . . significance of this
. . 1895. The present writer
. . . . his views upon this
. . . . . . : —

. . . . say that with this
. . . . history radically changed
. . . . marks the beginning of . .
. . . . the struggle is waged . .
. . . . the oriental nations themselves
. . . . sets of interests . . .
. which . . . . human progress
. . . .

WINE SHOP.

at its present stage and which are represented by the greatest Powers of the world. China's position as a dominant exclusive force was no sooner overthrown in Korea than it was replaced by that of another Power of a like policy and with aggressive tendencies. Moreover, the area opened to the advance of Russia covered not only Korea, but also northern China and beyond, and the new aggressor was the very Power which had thirty years before created a restless feeling among the Japanese by extending toward them through Primorsk and Saghalien its already enormous, contiguous dominion. The influence of Russia was now brought face to face with that of Japan, each with a promise to extend against, and perhaps to clash with, the other. With the movement of Russia there travelled from Europe to East Asia her sympathetic relations with France, while against this practical alliance stood the increasing common interests and sympathies of Japan, Great Britain and the United States; Germany remaining as a free lance between the two groups of Powers. This remarkable accession, in both area and agents, of the new activity in the East was heralded in, to all appearance, not gradually, but with a sudden sweep. And gravely ominous was its opening scene, representing at once a pretended good-will toward a feeble empire, and an armed coercion of a proud nation whom coercion would only stimulate to a greater ambition.

"It now remains for us to interpret the effects wrought upon Japan by the intervention of the three Powers, for the sentiment of the nation seems to be so universally and persistently misunderstood as to have caused even some of the natives to misconstrue their own feelings. It is generally supposed that the conduct of the Powers in depriving Japan of her prize of victory excited in her breast a deep feeling of revenge, but this view seems to evince too slight an understanding of the characteristics of the nation. Also, the prevailing sense of pity manifested by friendly foreigners toward Japan for her alleged misfortune appears entirely misplaced, for, on the contrary, she has derived an inestimable benefit from the experience. Let us explain. The most obvious

lesson drawn by the best minds of Japan and un-
consciously but deeply shared by the entire nation
was neither that the Powers were acting upon a
principle altogether different from their professed
motive, for that was too plain to every one ; nor
that she must some day humiliate the very Powers
which had brought coercion upon her, because it
was well known that their self-interest had demanded it, as hers would, were she in their place.
Japan suddenly awoke to an absorbing desire
which had little room for the question of a national
revenge. It became to her as clear as daylight
that the new position she had acquired in the
Orient by her victory over China could be maintained, and even her independence must be
guarded, only by an armament powerful enough to
give her a voice among the first Powers of the
world. If she would not retire into herself and
finally cease to exist, she must compete with the
greatest nations, not only in the arts of peace,
but also in those of war. Moreover, a far vaster
conflict than she had ever known in her history,
excepting the Mongol invasion of the thirteenth
century, was seen to be awaiting her future. It is

perhaps characteristic of modern Japan that she scarcely has time to breathe. The only course to save her seemed to be, now as at any other recent crisis of her life, to go forward and become equal to the new, expanding situation. As soon as her supremacy in the East was assured, Japan thus found herself confronted with a task hitherto almost unpremeditated, and henceforth began an enormous extension of her military forces, as well as a redoubled activity in all other lines of national progress.

"What is less obvious, but still more important, was — it is questionable if there is in the entire range of Japan's national life another point less understood abroad but more essential for an insight into the present and future of the extreme Orient than this — the increased enthusiasm of Japan in her ardent effort to strengthen her position in the world by basing her international conduct upon the fairest and best-tried principles of human progress. The effort is not free from occasional errors, but the large issue grows ever clearer in Japan's mind. A study of her past would seem to convince one with overwhelming evidence that her historic training has produced in Japan moral and material characteristics eminently fit for the pursuit of such policy. However that may be, the subsequent evolution of her interests at home and abroad seems, by a fortunate combination of circumstances, to have irrevocably committed her to this course; for not only does a common policy along these lines draw her and the Anglo-Saxon nations closer together, but it is therein also that the vital promise of her future appears to lie. And, it may be added, the consciousness of this powerful unity of moral and material life seems to have infused a thrilling new force into that historic love of the country of the Japanese nation. It is to the intervention of 1895 and the situation which ensued that Japan owes the hastening of all these results."

To return to the conduct of Russia. Having conferred a signal favour upon China by regaining for her the important territory of the Liao-tung, and by subsequently guaranteeing the Chinese loan of four hundred million francs raised mainly at Padis in order to pay a part of the indemnity due to Japan, Russia was not slow in obtaining from the grateful Court of Peking certain important privileges which all looked toward still greater ones to come. For instance, the Russo-Chinese Bank, which later proved to be an important commercial and political agent of the Russian Empire in the East, was organised in 1895; and a secret agreement or series of agreements, represented by the unconfirmed text of the notorious " Cassini Convention," was concluded between the Chinese and Russian Governments during 1896. It is idle to speculate on the contents of these agreements, for within two years hence all the more important points which could have been contained in them were incorporated in more definitely known Russo-Chinese conventions. Thus, in 1896, the Bank secured the right of building a railway across Manchuria in order to connect the trans-Baikal and South Ussuri lines of the Siberian Railway system. The concession was still further extended when, on March 27, 1898, Russia acquired a twenty-five-year lease of Port Arthur and Talien Wan and the right to connect these ports by rail with the trans-Manchurian line, the construction of which had been granted in 1896.

Closely preceded as it was by the German lease of Kiao-chau for ninety-nine years and also accompanied by similar concessions made by China to various other Powers, the Russian concession of 1898 just mentioned alone possessed a significance which made it a matter of the gravest concern. The control of Port Arthur would directly threaten the Chinese Capital, and ultimately imperil the safety of Korea. Moreover, by joining the leased ports with the Siberian Railway system, an effective connection would be established between the naval stations commanding the Yellow Sea and the immense land forces of the vast Russian Empire which was conterminous with China for thousands of miles. Over and above these considerations, it was apparent that, in order to connect Port Arthur and Vladivostok by sea, Russia would not rest satisfied until she should have acquired the southern coast of Korea, which contains harbours strategically superior to either of the ports in Russian possession. In 1898 Russia's determination to utilise the new concession to the utmost of its actual and prospective advantages was so great that the protests of the British

[167]

government against the lease of Port Arthur produced no impression upon her. As for Japan, — a Power which had three years before been forced out of the Liao-tung peninsula by the very Power which now secured its most strategic point, — it is remarkable that she neither was surprised at the outcome nor made an attempt to remonstrate against it.

The high-handed treatment, in 1898, of the Chinese Government by the Powers in their competition among themselves to establish their respective influence upon China's territory, greatly intensified the anti-foreign sentiment of her conservative people. The feeling at length broke out in a wide-spread insurrection in 1900, when the political designs of large secret societies and the ambition of certain intriguing members of the Imperial Court temporarily joined force under the rallying cry, "Save the dynasty and exterminate the foreigners!" It does not belong to us to relate the stirring events of the Boxer rising—the outrages on missionaries and murders of native Christians, the gallant defence of the foreigners besieged in Peking, the failure of the

a remonstrant against the lease of Port Arthur pre...
... ...no concession upon her. As for Japan,—
...Power which had three years before been forced
...out of the Liao-tung peninsula by the very Power
...who now seized its most strategic point,—it is
remarkable that she neither was surprised at the
outcome nor made an attempt to remonstrate
against it.

The high-handed treatment, in 1898, of the
Chinese Government by the Powers in their competition among themselves to establish their
respective influence upon China's territory,
greatly intensified the anti-foreign sentiment of
her conservative people. The feeling at length
broke out in a wide-spread insurrection in 1900,
when the political designs of large secret societies
and the ambition of certain intriguing members
of the Imperial Court temporarily joined forces
under the rallying cry, "Save the dynasty and
exterminate the foreigners!" It does not belong
to us to relate the stirring events of the Boxer
... —the outrages on missionaries and murders
of the native Christians, the gallant defence of the
... besieged in Peking, the failure of the

REELING SILK INTO LARGE SKEINS FOR THE MARKET.

international marine corps commanded by Admiral Seymour to reach the Capital, and the final relief of the Legations, on August 15, by the land forces of the allied Powers.

It will be remembered that, during the forced march of the allied troops toward Peking, and in the provisional administration of Tientsin and the Capital after their capture, the Japanese won universal admiration both for their discipline and courage and for their organising and executive power. The experience, indeed, was for them invaluable in enabling them to scrutinise at a close range the comparative capabilities of the soldiers of the civilised Powers, and to convince the sceptical world that Japan's arms were not after all uncontrollable by discipline nor her diplomacy by fair consideration of others' rights.

The Powers, too, were in their dealings with China obliged, under the necessity of the situation, to uphold a high principle which only two years before they seemed inclined so wantonly to disregard. We refer to the principle of the territorial integrity of the Chinese Empire. It is not strange that they should have, as they now did in 1900, repeatedly and unequivocally avowed their adherence to this fundamental idea, for otherwise a general partition and a consequent uprising and bloodshed throughout the vast empire would have been the result. A colossal revolution of the most ominous character was thus happily averted. It was just at this time, however, that Russia was silently but resolutely creating a situation in Manchuria which brought about a complete change of the diplomatic aspect of the far East. Russia had taken military possession of Manchuria. Under the plea that the Boxer outrages had spread from North China to Manchuria, where Russia possessed large vested interests, the latter poured into the territory large forces from Siberia and European Russia, and, by the time when the allied troops relieved Peking, had reduced the major part of the Three Provinces under her military occupation. The war of conquest — as it was openly called by some Russian authorities — continued till the close of 1900, until the government of the Czar completely mastered this territory of three hundred and sixty-four thousand square miles in extent. Meanwhile, the Russian diplomats at St. Petersburg and Peking were making their best effort to convince the other Powers that the Provinces would be restored to China as soon as normal peace returned, but that Russia's unique position justified her in dealing with the Manchurian question independently and without interference from others.

It was in the spirit of this latter point of her policy that Russia began, so early as at the end of 1900, to propose to the Chinese Government demands concerning Manchuria which were deemed by other Powers as hardly compatible with the territorial integrity of China and with an equal economic opportunity therein for all nations. The first reported demands almost amounted to the creation of a Russian protectorate in the Sheng-king Province of Manchuria; while the next ones, presented early in 1901, contemplated a similar arrangement regarding all Manchuria, besides the exclusion of the economic enterprises of other nations, not only from Manchuria, but also from Mongolia, Tarbagatai, Ili, Kashgar, Yarkand. Khotan, etc. When other

Powers, especially Japan, objected to the conclusion of such agreements, Count Lamsdorff, the Russian Foreign Minister, invariably explained that his government never departed from its firm resolution to restore Manchuria to China, and that it was desired simply to effect a provisional agreement with China pending the return of normal peace in the territory. Having, however, failed to come to a conclusion with the government of Peking, M. Lessar, the Russian Minister there, brought forward, late in 1901, new proposals, the comparatively lenient character of which seemed to commend itself to the feeble Foreign Office of China. Just at this juncture, the progress of Russian diplomacy regarding Manchuria was temporarily interrupted by the unexpected publication of the agreement of an Anglo-Japanese alliance concluded on January 30 and announced on February 12, 1902.

The consummation of this remarkable agreement may be said to have been due, not so much to the diplomatic tact, great as it was, of the Katsura Cabinet of Tokio, as to the increasingly common interests and common policy of Great Britain and Japan in China and Korea, and, what is equally important, to the recent conduct of Russia in Manchuria which seemed to threaten the general peace of the far East and endanger the interests of all concerned save Russia. The contracting parties mutually recognised the independence of China and Korea, and disavowed in those countries all aggressive designs. They also bound themselves, for a period fixed for five years but capable of prolongation, the one to be neutral should the other, under the necessity of protecting its threatened interests, engage in hostilities with another Power. If, however, the belligerent ally should be confronted in war by more than two Powers, the other ally should come in assistance and conduct hostilities in common. About a month after the publication of this Agreement, on March 16, the allied governments of Paris and St. Petersburg issued a Declaration that they were, as they had been hitherto, in perfect accord with the principles of the Agreement, but that they reserved to themselves the right to consult as to the

means of protecting their special interests in the
far East, if those interests should be menaced
by "either the aggressive action of third Powers,
or the recurrence of disturbances in China,
jeopardising the integrity and free development
of that Power." The Declaration and an accom-
panying Russian document specially emphasised
that the conclusion of the Anglo-Japanese
Agreement in no way changed the political
situation in the East, for France and Russia
found in the principles expounded by the other
allies regarding the integrity and the "open
door" of Korea and China the very ideas which
had always guided their own traditional policy
in those countries. Who could deny, however,
that the publication of the Agreement and
of the Declaration, the one so closely after the
other, had an effect of greatly clarifying the
political atmosphere of the East, as well as
accentuating the widening contrast between the
two different policies upheld by the two powerful coalitions?

Russia quickly followed these events by concluding with China, on April 8, 1902, the

celebrated convention providing for the evacuation of Manchuria within the next eighteen months, as follows : — from that part of the Sheng-king Province lying west of the Liao River, by October 8, 1902; from the rest of the Province and the entire Kirin Province, by April 8, 1903; and from the remaining Province of Hei-lung, by October 8, 1903. Thus after a year and a half the Three Eastern Provinces — as Manchuria is called by the Chinese — would be completely restored to the Chinese Empire, provided that other Powers should throw no obstacles in the way of Russia, and that China should effectively protect the Russian subjects and properties within the territory. These terms, in comparison with the more drastic of the former abortive demands, appeared very liberal on the part of Russia, but what hidden impediments against a real evacuation Russia deliberately placed between the lines of the Convention were soon to be discovered. The first of the three stipulated periods of evacuation ended on October 8, 1902, and the evacuation of the regions west of the Liao

[175]

took place even before the arrival of that date. Unfortunately for Russia, however, foreign travellers and diplomatic agents in Manchuria persistently reported that a large part of the alleged evacuation signified nothing more than the removal of Russian troops from Chinese towns to Russian quarters in Manchuria, while, besides, the continued existence of the "railway guards" numbering twenty-five or thirty thousand men stationed along the Manchurian railway would make even a real evacuation largely nominal.

When the end of the second period of evacuation, namely, April 8, 1902, drew near, not even the nominal withdrawal which was said to have characterised the first period of evacuation took place except in a few towns, but, on the contrary, M. Plançon, the Russian *Chargé d'Affaires* at Peking, was reported to have proposed new demands in seven articles. These articles included a pledge by China not to lease or sell any portion of whatever size in Manchuria to any other Power — a pledge naturally pointing toward the establishment

[176]

... the armed ...

... Russia, however, ...

... agents in M...

... that a large part ...

... making use ...

... troops from ...

... in Manchuria, ...

... of the railway

... five or thirty thousand

... Manchurian railway

... and evacuation largely

... the second period of

... 8, 1902, drew near,

... withdrawal which was said

... first period of evacua-

... in a few towns, but,

M. Plançon, the Russian

... at Peking, was reported to

... demands in seven articles.

... which a pledge by China not

... military portion of whatever size in

... to any other Power—a pledge

... toward the establishment

x

A GROUP OF NAVAL OFFICERS.

of a Russian protectorate in this vast territory; and the closing of Manchuria against the trade of any other nation, except at the already open port of Newchwang, where Russia demanded the perpetuation of the management of its customs-receipts by the Russo-Chinese Bank, — a stipulation by no means reconcilable with the principle of the equal economic opportunity for all nations. At the presentation of these demands, the educated classes of China seemed at last to have been aroused to an intense patriotic sentiment, for they petitioned the vacillating Court of Peking from all the eighteen Provinces to reject the Russian overtures. Of course, the British, American and Japanese Governments entered strong protests at the Foreign Office of China. The repeated refusal of the Peking Government to accede to the Muscovite demands seemed, however, to call forth from M. Lessar even heavier demands than before.

Just at this time, Russian relations with Korea had become even more critical than in Manchuria. In spite of the three agreements which Russia concluded with Japan in 1896 and 1898 regarding

Korea, M. Pavloff, the ambitious Russian Minister at Seul, together with certain semi-official Russian agents, continually embarrassed the Korean Government by presenting demands some of which seriously infringed the sovereign rights of the peninsular empire. Unfortunately, the Emperor proved conciliatory beyond the point of his own security, while his ministers were either too weak or too venal to resist the means employed by the Russians in their incessant effort to overthrow Japanese and establish Russian influence in Korea. There consequently proceeded at Seul the most strenuous diplomatic struggle between the Russian and Japanese representatives, every inch of the former's move being closely disputed or offset by the counter-move of the latter. The process was to the last degree exasperating to Japan, for she could object to Russian measures of aggression only through the utterly unreliable Korean Government which was never sufficiently alive to the urgent needs of Korea as a modern State. All these difficulties were brought to a climax when, from May, 1903, Russian troops began to arrive at Yongampo near the mouth of the Yalu River on

the northern frontier, ostensibly with a view to
protecting the timber land in the vicinity, and
proceeded to occupy large tracts of land and show
evident signs of a permanent possession and forti-
fication of the neighbouring district; when, simultaneously, the Russian garrisons at strategic points
on the Manchurian side of the Korean border were
strengthened, so that a military connection between the newly seized Yongampo and Liao-yang
and Port Arthur was fairly established; and when,
in the face of these grave circumstances, the
Korean Government proved impotent to stay
Russia's hands and even was divided against itself
in its opinion as to the legality of the Russian
conduct.

The intense irritation which these events caused
among the government and people of Japan may
well be imagined. It appeared to them that the
time had now at last arrived when the critical
situation should no longer be allowed to continue,
and when Japan should directly deal with Russia,
instead of protesting through the governments of
Peking and Seul so incapable of enforcing their
own rights. Accordingly, the responsible states-

[179]

men of Tokyo formulated, on June 23d, principles upon which negotiations with Russia should be based. Japan's wish to discuss with Russia the possibility of defining the mutual position of the two Powers in those parts of the East where their interests touched one another was assented to by Russia early in August. The way was thus opened for an amicable solution of the debatable questions the existence of which had so continually threatened the peace of the Orient.

It was, however, disheartening to see that in the meantime the political conditions at St. Petersburg had rapidly changed, a warlike faction largely overshadowing the peace party represented by M. Witte, Minister of Finance, and Count Lamsdorff, Minister for Foreign Affairs. The former was relieved of his office and transferred to the Presidency of the Council of State, and the latter, so far as the Eastern affairs were concerned, seemed to have lost the real control over the situation, which passed into the hands of Admiral Alexieff of Port Arthur. The Admiral was, on August 13, made Viceroy of the newly created province of the "Far East," and was vested with an immense authority over the military, naval, and diplomatic affairs of this important territory.

It was under these circumstances that the proposals of the Tokyo Government were, on August 12, presented to Count Lamsdorff by Mr. S. Kurino, the Japanese Minister at St. Petersburg. It is essential for any clear understanding of Japan's policy in the East to examine the precise nature of these proposals. They consisted of the following articles: (1) That both Powers should respect the independence and the territorial integrity of China and Korea, and maintain in those countries the principle of the equal opportunity for the commerce and industry of all nations, — it may be added that these were the cardinal principles of the Anglo-Japanese alliance, and that from them Japan would never depart on her initiative under any circumstance whatever; (2) that Russia should recognise Japan's preponderating interests in Korea, and Japan should likewise respect Russia's special interests in the railway enterprises in Manchuria; and that each Power should recognise the right of the other to take necessary measures to protect its interests in the respective territory, sub-

[181]

ject always, however, to the principles stated in the first Article; (3) that each Power should not impede the development (within limits consistent with the first Article) of the economic activity, of Japan in Korea, and of Russia in Manchuria; and that Russia should not obstruct the possible extension of the Korean railway into southern Manchuria, connecting it with the Manchurian and the Shanhaikwan-Newchwang railways; (4) that each Power should engage that, should it become necessary, in order to safeguard her interests, to despatch soldiers, — either Japan to Korea, or Russia to Manchuria, — the number of troops should not be larger than is necessary for the purpose, and that they should be withdrawn as soon as the end should be accomplished; (5) that Russia should recognise Japan's sole right, in the interest of reform and good government, to give to Korea advice and assistance, including necessary military support; and (6) that the present Agreement should supplant all the previous Russo-Japanese agreements regarding Korea.

To these proposals Russia did not reply until nearly eight weeks had passed. During this interval she proposed and Japan reluctantly agreed that negotiations should be conducted at Tokyo, instead of at St. Petersburg, and that the Japanese note and Russian counter-note should together form the basis of discussion, instead of the former alone, as had been requested by Japan. The significance of this move by Russia became apparent when her counter-proposals were received at Tokyo on October 8, followed by prolonged delays in her further replies.

The first Russian reply of October was a striking reminder that the government of the Czar was in no mood for meeting Japan's wishes, for its fundamental object was to exclude Manchuria from discussion, absolutely declining to recognise mutually with Japan China's sovereignty and open door therein. The reply, moreover, requested Japan to promise not to use any part of the Korean territory for any strategical purpose whatever, not to fortify the southern coast, and to consider the territory north of the thirty-ninth parallel — covering actually more than a third of the Korean Empire — as neutral between the two Powers. The inference was inevitable that Russia

[183]

was bent upon absorbing and closing all Manchuria, as well as marking out northern Korea as an eventual sphere of her influence, and that she was unwilling to recognise the supreme importance to Japan of the independence, strength and development of Korea. Indeed, the Russian representatives both at Peking and at Seul were reported to be, in spite of the negotiations pending between their government and the Japanese, simultaneously sharpening the tone of their aggressive diplomacy and exacting demands.

The position of Russia, however, so far as it concerned Manchuria, was rendered untenable by the conclusion, on October 8, of the new commercial treaties by China with Japan and with the United States. These treaties not only reinforced the sovereign rights of the Chinese Empire to deal with other independent Powers with respect to its own territory of Manchuria, but also emphasised anew the principle of the open door in that region by providing for the opening of three new ports to the world's trade —Mukden, the sepulchral city of the ruling dynasty, and Antung and Tatung-kao, near the

Korean border. It was evident to all observers
that the opening of these particular places was
justified, not so much by their actual commercial importance, as by the restraining effect
which the opening might have upon the aggressive policy of Russia. She, nevertheless, continued to strengthen her forces along the
Korean frontier, including the town of Antung,
and, before the end of October, suddenly seized
Mukden on a slight pretext.

The second Japanese note was communicated to
Russia on October 30, to which the latter replied
only on December 11. The third note of December 21 was, again, responded to on January 6,
1904. Throughout these notes and replies — the
exchange of which had now consumed, since
August last, five months so extremely trying on
the patience of Japan — both Powers maintained,
save in some minor points, the respective attitude
assumed in the first note and reply. It would
have been impossible for them to make the position of each clearer to the other than they had
already done, or to bring their opposing wishes an
inch nearer reconciliation. While, on the one

hand, the Japanese people were suffering from enormous economic losses arising from the extreme uncertainty of the Eastern situation, Russia, on the other hand, was increasing her military forces in the East on a stupendous scale, despatching since April, 1903, nineteen war vessels aggregating more than eighty-two thousand tons displacement, and forty thousand soldiers, besides two hundred thousand more who were about to be sent. These significant facts could scarcely be concealed from the eyes of the Japanese nation, who had now come to a profound conviction that, not only their material interests, but also their very national existence, was under a serious menace. It was, therefore, clearly against the wishes of the majority of the people that, on January 13, Baron J. Komura, the Foreign Minister, begged Russia, for the fourth time, to reconsider the grave situation in which both Powers found themselves. Instead of complying with Japan's repeated application for an early reply, Russia now greatly accelerated her military activity in the East. Thus, on January 21, numbers of infantry and artillery left Port Arthur and Dalny for the Korean frontier, followed by further reinforcements from the stronghold of Liao-yang; on the 28th, the troops on the Yalu were ordered by Viceroy Alexieff to be placed on the war footing; four days later the Commander of Vladivostok warned the Japanese Commercial Agent at the port to prepare for withdrawing his countrymen to Habarofsk, as he had received instructions from his government and was ready at any time to proclaim martial law; and, on February 8, all the Russian war vessels at Port Arthur, excepting the one under repair, steamed out of the harbour.

It now appeared to the Japanese Government that a further delay would be disastrous, and that the critical moment for decisive action had at last arrived. On February 5, at 2 P.M., therefore, Baron Komura wired two notes to the Russian Foreign Office through Mr. Kurino, the one breaking off the negotiations with Russia which had become useless, and the other severing all diplomatic relations with her which had lost their proper value. Japan's intention to take an independent course of action in order to protect her position and interests threatened by Russia was also announced in these notes. Mr. Kurino placed these communications in the hands of the surprised Count Lamsdorff at 4 P. M., February 6. The first act of war occurred at Chemulpo on the 8th, and hostilities were formally declared by the Emperors of Russia and Japan two days later. Diplomacy had failed, and war had begun in grim earnest. Immensely large issues are at this moment being fought out by fire and sword, and no one would dare prophesy the outcome of a war in which the belligerents are deliberately preparing themselves for a long, bitter struggle.

We should not, however, omit a few facts of great importance which have made Japan's policy in the East unmistakable beyond all cavil. As soon as the war began, the Japanese Government informed other Powers, on February 9, that it had, after a careful consideration, advised China to observe a strict neutrality throughout hostilities. Three days later, the circular note of Secretary Hay reached Tokyo, urging on the Powers the advisability of respecting the neutral rights and the administrative entity of China. Soon afterward Baron Komura made an explicit declaration to

China that Japan would not, as a result of the war, encroach upon the sovereignty and integrity of the Chinese Empire in Manchuria. This declaration was followed by the conclusion of an Agreement with Korea, by which Japan pledged herself to guarantee the independence and integrity of Korea and the safety of her reigning House, Korea in return promising to accept Japan's advice and assistance in the cause of her own reform and good government.

APPENDIX

APPENDIX

CORRESPONDENCE REGARDING THE NEGOTIATIONS BETWEEN JAPAN AND RUSSIA

1903 – 1904

Presented to the Imperial Diet, March, 1904

EXPLANATORY SPEECH OF THE MINISTER OF STATE FOR FOREIGN AFFAIRS

THE FOLLOWING IS AN ACCURATE TRANS– lation of the speech delivered by Baron Komura in the House of Representatives on the 23d instant : —

GENTLEMEN : — It is a great honour to me to make a brief statement before this House regarding the course of negotiations between Japan and Russia from the commencement to their termination. These negotiations lasted for more than half a year and are of a most complicated nature. Now I will try to briefly explain to you, gentlemen, the main points of these negotiations.

When, upon the sudden outbreak in North China of the Boxer troubles in 1900, the Powers sent forces to

APPENDIX

Chihli for the relief of their representatives and nationals, and were taking action in harmonious co-operation, Russia despatched a large army into Manchuria and finally took possession of the whole of that province. She repeatedly declared at the time that this despatch of troops was simply for suppressing the Chinese insurgents, and that she was determined to respect the sovereignty and territorial integrity of China in Manchuria, and that consequently her occupation of that province, which was the result of inevitable circumstances, was intended to be merely temporary. Nevertheless, on more than one occasion she tried to induce China to conclude a treaty of a nature tending to impair China's sovereignty and incompatible with the treaty rights of the Powers. Accordingly, on each occasion the Imperial Government warned both Russia and China, and Russia finally concluded, in April, 1902, a convention providing for the restoration of Manchuria. In accordance with the stipulations of the convention, Russia commenced to prepare for the restoration, and, in fact, a partial evacuation had already been effected, when in April last year there was a sudden change in her attitude, and not only were the withdrawal of her forces from Manchuria and the restitution of the administration to China suspended, but also various additional conditions were demanded from China. This action is believed to have been due to divided counsels in Russian Government circles regarding the solution of the Manchurian question, and to the subsequent ascendency of the party in favour of permanent occupation.

EXPLANATORY SPEECH

The development of affairs in Manchuria received the most careful attention at the hands of the Imperial Government. The maintenance of the independence and territorial integrity of Korea is of the utmost importance to the safety and repose of this empire and is in fact our traditional policy; while in the event of the absorption of Manchuria by Russia, the separate existence of Korea would be constantly menaced and the firm establishment of peace in the far East would become impossible. The Imperial Government, therefore, having regard to the future well-being of the empire, deemed it necessary for consolidating the peace of the extreme East and for securing the rights and interests of the empire to open, as soon as possible, negotiations with Russia with a view to a friendly definition of the interests of the two countries in Manchuria and Korea where those interests meet, and thereby to remove every cause of future conflict between Japan and Russia. The Japanese Government, therefore, instructed their representative at St. Petersburg on July 28, 1903, to bring their wishes to the attention of the Russian Government and to request the latter's concurrence. The Russian Government willingly assented, and the Russian Minister for Foreign Affairs announced that he had obtained Imperial authority to open negotiations on the subject. Accordingly, on the 12th of August last, the Imperial Government presented to the Russian Government through their minister at St. Petersburg, as a basis of negotiations, proposals substantially as follows:

1. Mutual engagement to respect the independence and territorial integrity of China and Korea.

APPENDIX

2. Mutual engagement to maintain the principle of equal opportunity for the commerce and industry of all nations in China and Korea.

3. Reciprocal recognition of Japan's preponderating interests in Korea and Russia's special interests in railway enterprises in Manchuria, and mutual recognition of the respective rights of Japan and Russia to take measures necessary for the protection of the above-mentioned interests so far as they do not conflict with the principle of Article I and Article II.

4. Recognition by Russia of the exclusive right of Japan to give advice and assistance to Korea in the interests of reform and good government.

5. Engagement on the part of Russia not to impede the eventual extension of the Korean railway into southern Manchuria so as to connect with the East China and the Shanhaikwan-Newchwang lines.

About ten days after the presentation of the proposals of which the above are essential points, the Russian Minister for Foreign Affairs suddenly suggested the transfer of the seat of negotiations to Tokyo. The Imperial Government, however, not only from the consideration that the progress of the negotiations would be facilitated by conducting them at the Russian capital, but also in view of the changes effected in the Russian administrative organisation in Manchuria and the erection of a viceroyalty of the far East, apprehended that the transfer of the seat of negotiations to Tokyo would not conduce to a satisfactory understanding. They accordingly repeatedly objected to the proposed transfer, but the Russian Minister for Foreign Affairs was insistent, assigning as the reason for his attitude the Czar's contemplated trip abroad, etc. Again, when the Imperial Government requested the Russian Minister for Foreign Affairs to accept in principle our proposals as a basis of negotiation, he only agreed to take them in conjunction with the Russian Counter-Proposals as such basis. The Imperial Government, deeming it disadvantageous to delay any longer the opening of discussions, agreed at length to transfer the seat of negotiations, and requested the Russian Government to present as soon as possible their Counter-Proposals. It was not until nearly a month later, the 3d of October, that the said Counter-Proposals were presented.

In those Counter-Proposals Russia, while having no objection to engage to respect the independence and territorial integrity of Korea, declined to extend the same engagement to China, and, so far from consenting to recognise the principle of equal opportunity for the commerce and industry of all nations in that country, requested Japan to acknowledge Manchuria and its littoral as entirely outside her sphere of interest. She further proposed various restrictions upon Japan's freedom of action in Korea; for instance while recognising Japan's right to despatch troops, when necessary, for the protection of her interests in Korea, Russia demanded previous notice in case of such despatch, and she refused to allow Japan to use any portion of Korean territory for strategical purposes. She went so far, in fact, as to propose to establish a neutral zone covering all Korean territory

APPENDIX

north of the 39th parallel, that is to say, more than one-third of the entire Korean Empire.

But, as the maintenance of the sovereignty and territorial integrity of China in Manchuria is absolutely essential to the preservation of the independence of Korea, and as such maintenance was none other than a principle which had been voluntarily and repeatedly declared by Russia herself, and moreover as it was considered necessary to keep uninjured the commercial interests of all the Powers concerned, upon the strength of the Russian engagement to respect treaty rights, the Imperial Government decided to maintain to the end their proposal on that subject, and necessary amendments to other Articles were also made. For instance, the imposition of any restriction on Japan in sending troops to Korea should be struck out. A neutral zone, if it was to be created, should be established on both sides of the boundary line between Manchuria and Korea with the same extent either way — i. e., fifty kilometres on each side. With these amendments several interviews took place with Baron Rosen from the 6th of October last, and as the result of repeated discussions, in which some of our amendments were accepted while as to others no agreement was arrived at, our definitive amendments were presented to Baron Rosen on the 30th of that month, and the Russian Government were asked to consider them. Although we frequently pressed for an answer, the Russian reply was again greatly delayed and it only reached us on the 11th of December. This embodied the 2d Russian Counter-Proposals. If the regret of the Imperial Government at such delay was deep, their disappointment at the contents of the reply, when it was received, was still more profound, for in it the clauses relating to Manchuria were completely suppressed, thus restricting the proposed convention entirely to Korea, while on the other hand the original demands regarding the neutral zone and the non-employment of Korean territory for strategical purposes were again revived. But the object of the convention was, as above stated, the removal of all causes of future conflict by a definitive settlement of all questions between the two countries at points where their interests meet, and if Manchuria were placed outside the purview of the arrangement, and a moiety of the problem were thus to remain unsolved, the result would plainly be at variance with the aims for which the negotiations were inaugurated. Consequently, on the 21st of December last, the Imperial Government asked the Government of Russia to reconsider their position on the subject of Manchuria, and again requested, with respect to Korea, the suppression of the restrictions as to the employment of Korean territory, and they also proposed the entire deletion of the clause relating to a neutral zone, as it was considered that, if Russia would not agree to its extension into Manchuria, it would be only fair not to create it in Korea.

The Russian Government gave their reply on the 6th of January, in which they still adhered to their original proposals as regards Korea, and on condition that those proposals were accepted by the Imperial Government they offered to agree to the insertion of a clause stipulating that Russia would not impede the enjoyment by Japan and other Powers of the rights and privileges acquired under existing treaties with China. This at first sight might seem to be a concession on the part of Russia regarding Manchuria, but in reality it was not so, for Russia made it conditional on certain propositions regarding Korea to which Japan could never agree. Again, no stipulations were to be made as to the territorial integrity of Manchuria, and the above-mentioned clause, unaccompanied by assurances concerning territorial integrity, would be practically valueless. Accordingly, the Imperial Government, recognising the absolute necessity of causing Russia to engage herself to respect the territorial integrity of Manchuria, and finding no margin for further concession in regard to Korea, decided to firmly insist upon their amendments, and once more requested on the 13th of January last, reconsideration by the Russian Government. They subsequently repeatedly instructed the Japanese Minister at St. Petersburg to ask for a reply. The Russian Government, however, did not give any answer, neither did the Russian Minister for Foreign Affairs, in his interview with Mr. Kurino, held so late as the 31st of January, afford even an indication as to the date whereon the reply would be presented.

Upon the whole, while the Imperial Government invariably met Russia in a conciliatory and frank spirit, in the hope of arriving at a speedy solution of the situation by yielding to Russia's wishes so far as they could do so without impairing the vital interests of Japan, Russia always unduly delayed her replies, or proposed such amendments as were altogether inconsistent with the idea of an amicable settlement, thus making the situation more and more complicated. Besides, Russia, while professing peaceful intentions on the one hand, made on the other great naval and military preparations, despatching all her most powerful war vessels to the extreme Orient, and sending military reinforcements, tens of thousands strong, to Manchuria and the neighbouring regions. Unusually great activity was shown by her in purchasing and transporting arms, ammunition, stores and coal to the same region, so that it was placed beyond the range of doubt that Russia had no sincere desire for conciliation, and only aimed at compelling us to yield to her designs by force of arms. Especially towards the end of January the warlike activities of Russia were so far accelerated that, had Japan permitted any further procrastination, the empire would certainly have been placed in serious danger. Although the Imperial Government entertained a most sincere desire for peace, yet in the face of such circumstances they could not avoid deciding, after a full and careful survey of the situation, to break off the negotiations with Russia and to take all necessary measures for self-defence. Accordingly, on the 5th of February, they issued telegraphic instructions to the Japanese Minister at St. Petersburg to announce to the Russian Government that the Imperial Government had terminated negotiations relative to the proposed Russo-Japanese convention; that they would take such independent action as they might deem best to defend and consolidate their menaced position and to protect their established rights and legitimate interests, and that they would sever diplomatic relations with Russia and withdraw their Legation. In accordance with those instructions our

APPENDIX

minister at St. Petersburg made the communication on the 6th of February last.

Such is, gentlemen, a brief account of the negotiations with Russia. As for the details, the document just presented to the Diet will afford you full information.

.

CORRESPONDENCE

No. 1 — *Baron Komura to Mr. Kurino.*

Токyo, July 28, 1903.

(Telegram.)

THE JAPANESE GOVERNMENT HAVE OB-
served with close attention the development of affairs
in Manchuria, and they view with grave concern the present
situation there. So long as there were grounds for hope that
Russia would carry out her engagement to China and her
assurances to other Powers on the subject of the evacuation
of Manchuria, the Japanese Government maintained an attitude of watchful reserve. But the recent action of Russia
in formulating new demands in Peking and in consolidating rather than relaxing her hold on Manchuria compels
belief that she has abandoned the intention of retiring from
Manchuria, while her increased activity along the Korean
frontier is such as to raise doubts regarding the limits of her
ambition. The unrestrained permanent occupation of Manchuria by Russia would create a condition of things prejudicial to the security and interest of Japan. Such occupation
would be destructive of the principle of equal opportunity
and in impairment of the territorial integrity of China.
But, what is of still more serious moment to the Japanese
Government, Russia stationed on the flank of Korea would

[203]

be a constant menace to the separate existence of that empire, and in any event it would make Russia the dominant power in Korea. Korea is an important outpost in Japan's line of defence, and Japan consequently considers the independence of Korea absolutely essential to her own repose and safety. Japan possesses paramount political as well as commercial and industrial interests and influence in Korea, which, having regard to her own security, she cannot consent to surrender to, or share with, any other Power. The Japanese Government have given the matter their most serious consideration and have resolved to approach the Russian Government in a spirit of conciliation and frankness with a view to the conclusion of an understanding designed to compose questions which are at this time the cause of just and natural anxiety; and, in the estimation of the Japanese Government, the moment is opportune for making the attempt to bring about the desired adjustment.

The Japanese Government, reposing confidence in your judgment and discretion, have decided to place these delicate negotiations in your hands. It is the wish of the Japanese Government to place their present invitation to the Russian Government entirely on an official footing, and you are accordingly instructed to open the question by presenting to Count Lamsdorff a Note Verbale to the following effect:

"The Imperial Japanese Government, believing that the Imperial Russian Government share with them the desire to remove from the relations of the two empires every cause of future misunderstanding, would be glad to enter with the Imperial Russian Government upon examination of the condition of affairs in the extreme East where their interests meet, with a view to a definition of their respective special interests in those regions. If, as is confidently hoped, this suggestion meets approval in principle, the Imperial Japanese Government will be prepared to present to the Imperial Russian Government their views as to the nature and scope of the proposed understanding."

In presenting the foregoing note to Count Lamsdorff, you will be careful to make him understand that our purposes are entirely friendly, but that we attach great importance to the subject. You will present the note to Count Lamsdorff as soon as possible, and keep me fully informed regarding the steps taken by you under this instruction ; and immediately upon the receipt of an affirmative reply from the Russian Government, the substance of our proposals will be telegraphed to you.

No. 2 — *Mr. Kurino to Baron Komura.*

PETERSBURG, July 31, 1903.
Received, August 2, 1903.

(Telegram.)

YOUR Excellency's telegram of the 28th instant was duly received. In accordance with the instructions contained therein, I saw Count Lamsdorff to-day and, before handing to His Excellency the Note Verbale, I stated substantially as follows : —

"The condition of affairs in the far East is becoming more and more complicated, and unless something be done at present with the view of removing all causes of misunderstanding between Japan and Russia, the relations of the two countries will increase in difficulty, entailing nothing but disadvantages to both countries. Under the circumstances, the Imperial Government, fully animated by a spirit of frankness and conciliation, have decided to approach the Imperial Russian Government with a view to arrive at an understanding."

I then handed to him the Note Verbale, saying that I was so instructed. After he had seen it, I expressed my ardent hope that the Russian Government would share the above view in the same spirit. Count Lamsdorff said that he was perfectly satisfied with the decision of the Japanese Government, for, as he had said to me very often, an understanding between the two countries is not only desirable, but is the best policy; should Russia and Japan enter into full understanding, no one would in future attempt to sow the seeds of discord between the two countries. So far as he was concerned, he was, he said, in perfect accord with the view of the Japanese Government; but he wished to see the Emperor on the subject before a definite answer was given. He expects to see the Emperor next Tuesday, and he promised to give me an answer on the following day. He added that the Emperor would surely approve the matter.

No. 8 — *Baron Komura to Mr. Kurino.*

TOKYO, August 3, 1903.

(Telegram.)

IN reference to my telegram of the 28th of July, the Japanese Government, after giving most serious consideration to the condition of affairs in those centres where the interests of the two Powers meet, have decided to propose the following as the basis of an understanding between Japan and Russia.

"1. Mutual engagement to respect the independence and territorial integrity of the Chinese and Korean Empires and to maintain the principles of equal opportunity for the commerce and industry of all nations in those countries.

"2. Reciprocal recognition of Japan's preponderating interests in Korea and Russia's special interests in railway enterprises in Manchuria, and of the right of Japan to take in Korea and of Russia to take in Manchuria such measures as may be necessary for the protection of their respective interests as above defined, subject, however, to the provisions of Article I of this agreement.

"3. Reciprocal undertaking on the part of Russia and Japan not to impede development of those industrial and commercial activities respectively of Japan in Korea and of Russia in Manchuria, which are not inconsistent with the stipulations of Article I of this agreement.

"Additional engagement on the part of Russia not to impede the eventual extension of the Korean railway into southern Manchuria so as to connect with the East China and Shanhaikwan-Newchwang lines.

"4. Reciprocal engagement that in case it is found necessary to send troops by Japan to Korea, or by Russia to Manchuria, for the purpose either of protecting the interests mentioned in Article II of this agreement, or of suppressing insurrection or disorder calculated to create international complications, the troops so sent are in no case to exceed the actual number required and are to be forthwith recalled as soon as their missions are accomplished.

" 5. Recognition on the part of Russia of the exclusive right of Japan to give advice and assistance in the interest of reform and good government in Korea, including necessary military assistance.

" 6. This agreement to supplant all previous arrangements between Japan and Russia respecting Korea."

In handing the foregoing project to Count Lamsdorff, you will say that it is presented for the consideration of the Russian Government in the firm belief that it may be found to serve as a basis upon which to construct satisfactory arrangement between the two governments, and you will assure Count Lamsdorff that any amendment or suggestion he may find it necessary to offer will receive the immediate and friendly consideration of the Japanese Government. It will not be necessary for you to say much in elucidation of the separate items of the project, as they are very largely self-explanatory ; but you might point out that the project taken as a whole will be found to be but little more than the logical and essential development and extension of the principles already recognised by the two governments, or of conditions embodied in the engagements which the project is designed to supplant.

The foregoing instruction is sent to you in anticipation that the answer to the Note Verbale presented by you will be favourable ; but you will not act on that instruction until you receive further instructions, which will be given after you have communicated to me the answer to the Note Verbale.

CORRESPONDENCE

No. 4 — *Mr. Kurino to Baron Komura.*

PETERSBURG, August 5, 1903.
Received, August 6, 1903.

(Telegram.)

COUNT LAMSDORFF says he is authorised by the Emperor to open negotiations with me on the subject of the Note Verbale.

No. 5 — *Baron Komura to Mr. Kurino.*

TOKYO, August 6, 1903.

(Telegram.)

IN reference to your telegrams dated the 31st ultimo and 5th instant, you will state to Count Lamsdorff that the Imperial Government fully appreciate the friendly spirit with which the Russian Government received the proposal of the Japanese Government to enter upon negotiations with regard to an understanding between the two countries, and then present at once the project to the Russian Government in accordance with instructions contained in my telegram of the 3d instant.

No. 6 — *Mr. Kurino to Baron Komura.*

PETERSBURG, August 12, 1903.
Received, August 14, 1903.

(Telegram.)

COUNT LAMSDORFF, being now very much occupied, could not receive me until to-day, when I handed to His Excellency the proposed project in English in accordance with your instructions. I added that the longer the conclusion of an accord is postponed the more difficult will it become, as the condition of affairs in the far East is now getting more and more complicated. I asked him to hasten the matter as much as possible. He said he would examine the project with care.

No. 7 —*Mr. Kurino to Baron Komura.*

PETERSBURG, August 24, 1903.
Received, August 25, 1903.

(Telegram.)

COUNT LAMSDORFF received me yesterday by special arrangement, and I asked his views, as well as the attitude of the Russian Government regarding our proposals, adding that the Japanese Government are now impatiently waiting for a reply. He said that he had studied the project seriously, but that the Emperor having been absent over a week on account of the manœuvres, he had been unable to take any steps in the matter; but he asked my opinion about transferring the negotiations to Tokyo, as there were many details which would have to be referred to Admiral Alexieff. I said to him that the Japanese Government having confided the matter to me, I should prefer to proceed with it, but that I was willing to communicate his opinion to you.

He stated that he has already sent copy of our project to Port Arthur with the view of obtaining the opinion of Admiral Alexieff. After such conversation, he said the question . of Japanese railway enterprise in Manchuria would be difficult, but upon all other points perhaps the Russian Government would be able to come to an understanding. I said that in order to arrive at a satisfactory understanding, mutual concessions as well as a spirit of conciliation are necessary, and that the Japanese Government would be prepared to give favourable consideration if any suggestions should be made by Count Lamsdorff.

No. 8 — *Baron Komura to Mr. Kurino.*

TOKYO, August 26, 1903.

(Telegram.)

IN reference to your telegram of the 24th instant, you will say to Count Lamsdorff that the Japanese Government would prefer to continue negotiations in St. Petersburg, believing that by so doing, the work will be greatly facilitated. You can add that there are no details to be considered in connection with pending negotiations which require local knowledge, and that the Japanese Government, having placed the negotiation in your hand, would dislike to make any change. You will say to Count Lamsdorff that the Japanese Government are anxiously awaiting a definite reply from his government to their proposals, and you will continue to use every endeavour to obtain from him such a reply as soon as possible.

No. 9 — *Mr. Kurino to Baron Komura.*

PETERSBURG, August 27, 1903.
Received, August 28, 1903.

(Telegram.)

I SAW Count Lamsdorff to-day on the subject of your telegram dated the 26th instant. He said he had audience of the Emperor last Tuesday, and was told that His Majesty desires very much the early conclusion of an *entente* satisfactory for both countries, and expressed his wish to conduct the negotiations at Tokyo so as to expedite the matter. Then Count Lamsdorff added that the Emperor is to leave here for the country next Monday, and then for foreign countries for some time, and at the same time the ministers concerned would be absent from St. Petersburg. Consequently, negotiations in Tokyo would be much the easier and quicker way of concluding the matter. I said, referring to my conversation with Count Lamsdorff of the 23d instant, that the proposed understanding involved mostly questions of principles and politics rather than details, and consequently that the continuation of negotiations at St. Petersburg would be proper and at the same time the quickest way to arrive at a satisfactory understanding. He repeated what he had just said and insisted upon his proposition.

Under the circumstances, I think it hardly possible to change the course now proposed by Count Lamsdorff under authority of the Emperor. I also think that negotiations at Tokyo would entail many disadvantageous consequences; and definite instruction for the further course is awaited.

No. 10 — *Baron Komura to Mr. Kurino.*

TOKYO, August 29, 1903.

(Telegram.)

IN reference to your telegram of the 27th instant, you will say to Count Lamsdorff that the Japanese Government still think that negotiation will be facilitated if continued in St. Petersburg since the negotiations relate to principles and not details; and you will add that he and you having been duly authorised in the matter, and the proposals of Japan having been presented to him, the Japanese Government had supposed that the seat of negotiation had been agreed to. You will accordingly urge upon Count Lamsdorff the desire of the Japanese Government to continue the negotiations in St. Petersburg, and express a hope that his government will reconsider the question. You will also say that the Japanese Government presume they are justified in assuming from the proposal to transfer negotiations to Tokyo, that our proposals are in principle acceptable to the Russian Government as the basis of negotiations.

No. 11 — *Mr. Kurino to Baron Komura.*

PETERSBURG, August 31, 1903.
Received, September 2, 1903.

(Telegram.)

I SAW Count Lamsdorff to-day and explained fully the purport of your telegram of the 29th instant. The substance of his reply is as follows : —

He said that the negotiations relate to principles, but principles must be decided upon examination of local and practical questions. Accordingly the Russian Government desired to transfer the discussions to Tokyo on account of the necessity of consultation with Admiral Alexieff, and also to manifest a sense of deference to Japan as the proposal had been made by her, and that the acceptance of the proposal at St. Petersburg does not signify that the seat of negotiations should be at the same place. He added that the proposal to transfer the negotiations to Tokyo does not necessarily mean that our proposals are accept-

APPENDIX

able to the Russian Government, as bases for negotiations could not be determined without reference to practical questions, concerning which Baron Rosen and Admiral Alexieff have much better knowledge than he himself.

I urged as my opinion that this being the most important question of high politics between our two countries, perhaps the Emperor had much to decide, and consequently it would be very convenient if the negotiations were conducted at St. Petersburg, and wished his serious reconsideration of the question of transfer as such reconsideration is much desired by the Japanese Government. I objected also to the suggestion of transfer on the ground that the question relates to principles as well as to the direction of international political concerns which may not be within the powers conferred upon Admiral Alexieff. If I remember rightly, I said, I understand that his authority is limited to mere questions of local administration. He said that on this question Admiral Alexieff would only be consulted and decide nothing, and added that he, Count Lamsdorff, is also desirous to settle the question as quickly as possible, and that is the reason why he suggested the transfer. The Russian Counter-Proposals are being prepared by persons having local knowledge, consequently the transfer of negotiations to Tokyo would expedite the matter. Should the negotiations be conducted at St. Petersburg, he would be obliged to attend to the matter personally with me; but this autumn he has to be long absent from the city on account of his attendance upon the Emperor. In case of his journey to Vienna and Rome, he may also visit a certain foreign country and would be liable to be frequently interrupted in the negotiations. But in case of negotiations at Tokyo, he could direct them by telegraph, and telegrams from Tokyo could always follow him wherever he might happen to be; besides, he said, as we know very well, the Russian way of conducting business here is not very expeditious. At the conclusion, he said he is to have audience of the Emperor to-day, and will explain to him the reasons why an early understanding between the two countries is desirable as mentioned by me; and he promised to repeat to His Majesty the special desire of the Japanese Government to conduct the negotiations at St. Petersburg; but he added that no change of view on the subject could be expected.

No. 12 — *Baron Komura to Mr. Kurino.*

Tokyo, September 2, 1903.

(Telegram.)

In reference to your telegram of the 31st ultimo, you will say to Count Lamsdorff that it being the acknowledged desire of both Powers to arrive at an understanding as soon as possible, the Japanese Government fear that discussions would be greatly protracted if the negotiations were now to be transferred to Tokyo without some accepted basis for negotiations; and you will add that the Japanese Government, having presented their proposals in concrete form to the Russian Government, believe that negotiations, wherever conducted, would be greatly facilitated if the Russian Government were primarily to announce whether such proposals can in principle be accepted as the basis for negotiations. The Japanese Government do not understand that the acceptance of those proposals as such basis would exclude amendments that might be regarded as necessary. On the contrary, such acceptance would merely fix a definite point of departure, which is desirable in all negotiations and very important in the present case. You will use every endeavour to secure the desired announcement from the Russian Government.

No. 13 — *Mr. Kurino to Baron Komura.*

St. Petersburg, September 5, 1903.
Received, September 6, 1903.

(Telegram.)

I saw Count Lamsdorff yesterday. With the view of preventing any misunderstanding about the sense of the instruction contained in your telegram of the 2d instant, and also with the view of impressing upon the Russian Government the feeling of importance placed by the Japanese Government on the matter, I prepared a Note Verbale which I handed to him. We then had a rather prolonged discussion on the question. The substance of his remarks is as follows:—

According to his experience of forty years in the Foreign Office, negotiations of an international character had always been conducted on the proposals of one Power together with the reply of the other, and it was not usual to accept the proposition of one Power as the sole basis of negotiations. Baron Rosen had already been commanded by the Emperor to study seriously the proposition of the Japanese Government, and at the same time to prepare and elaborate Counter-Proposals in consultation with Admiral Alexieff, and, if the

Japanese Government were willing to enter into negotiation, to commence immediately the *pour-parlers* adopting the propositions of the Japanese Government and the Russian Counter-Proposals as the basis of negotiations. I said during the discussion that if the Russian Government were really animated by a desire to enter into a satisfactory arrangement with Japan, I should deem it highly necessary that the Russian Government should instruct their negotiators to adopt as the basis the Japanese proposals, or at least the essential principles thereof, so as to facilitate the attainment of the object of the negotiation, for I am inclined to doubt if Admiral Alexieff is disposed to enter into negotiations with, Japan in a spirit of conciliation, which is of prime necessity in order to arrive at a satisfactory understanding. He said that when he received our project there were only two courses open for Russia to take, either to reject our proposals or to enter into negotiations on them. The Russian Government have adopted the latter course; this does not, however, signify acceptance of our project in its entirety or in principles; but having agreed to the proposition to enter into an *entente*, they have decided to examine the propositions and to prepare Counter-Proposals so that the two might be used as the basis of negotiations. Besides he said that in our project there are certain clauses which could not be reconciled with Russian interests, and others which require modifications; and he could not say that the Russian Government accepted our proposals even in principle as basis, but only in conjunction with their Counter-Proposals.

[217]

APPENDIX

Having exhausted every effort for the attainment of the desire of the Japanese Government, I am now fully convinced that it will not be possible to change the course proposed by Count Lamsdorff; and I think that there is no other way for Japan but to agree to his suggestion. Count Lamsdorff is to leave here on the 10th instant for Darmstadt to attend the Emperor of Russia.

No. 14 — *Baron Komura to Mr. Kurino.*

TOKYO, September 9, 1903.

(Telegram.)

IN reference to your telegram of the 5th instant, you are hereby instructed to inform Count Lamsdorff that the Japanese Government consent to transfer negotiations to Tokyo, and you will add that the Japanese Government trust that instructions to the Russian Minister at Tokyo are of such a character as to enable him to present the Russian Counter-Proposals without delay and to proceed immediately with the negotiations.

No. 15 — *Mr. Kurino to Baron Komura.*

PETERSBURG, September 9, 1903.
Received, September 10, 1903.

(Telegram.)

I SAW Count Lamsdorff to-day. He said Baron Rosen and Admiral Alexieff have already been instructed by telegraph, by order of the Emperor, to prepare the Counter-Proposals as quickly as possible, and to commence negotiations at the earliest date, and he does not think it necessary to repeat the same instructions.

CORRESPONDENCE

No. 16 — *Baron Komura to Mr. Kurino.*

TOKYO, September 24, 1903.

(Telegram.)

BARON ROSEN left Tokyo on the 22d instant for Port Arthur. Previously to his departure, he called on me and told me that he had been instructed under Imperial order some time ago to hold himself ready to start at once for Port Arthur, whenever necessity might arise to do so, in order to expedite the preparation of the Russian Counter-Proposals between Admiral Alexieff and himself, and that he had just received from the Admiral a request to repair to Port Arthur for personal consultation on the subject. He added that he expected to come back within about eleven days.

No. 17 — *Baron Komura to Mr. Kurino.*

TOKYO, October 5, 1903.

(Telegram.)

BARON ROSEN came back to Tokyo on the 3d instant. He called on me on the same day and handed to me the following as the Russian Counter-Proposals, which, he said, was sanctioned by the Emperor of Russia, upon joint presentation by Admiral Alexieff and himself: —

1. Mutual engagement to respect the independence and territorial integrity of the Korean Empire.

2. Recognition by Russia of Japan's preponderating interests in Korea and of the right of Japan to give advice and assistance to Korea tending to improve the civil administration of the empire without infringing the stipulations of Article I.

[219]

APPENDIX

3. Engagement on the part of Russia not to impede the commercial and industrial undertakings of Japan in Korea, nor to oppose any measures taken for the purpose of protecting them so long as such measures do not infringe the stipulations of Article I.

4. Recognition of the right of Japan to send for the same purpose troops to Korea, with the knowledge of Russia, but their number not to exceed that actually required, and with the engagement on the part of Japan to recall such troops as soon as their mission is accomplished.

5. Mutual engagement not to use any part of the territory of Korea for strategical purposes nor to undertake on the coasts of Korea any military works capable of menacing the freedom of navigation in the Straits of Korea.

6. Mutual engagement to consider that part of the territory of Korea lying to the north of the 39th parallel as a neutral zone into which neither of the Contracting Parties shall introduce troops.

7. Recognition by Japan of Manchuria and its littoral as in all respects outside her sphere of interest.

8. This agreement to supplant all previous agreements between Russia and Japan respecting Korea.

No. 18 — *Baron Komura to Mr. Kurino.*

TOKYO, October 8, 1903.

(Telegram.)

IN reference to my telegram of the 5th instant, I have begun discussion with the Russian Minister to Japan taking our proposals and the Russian Counter-Proposals as the basis and with a view to secure, if possible, the recognition by Russia of the fundamental principles laid down in our proposals.

No. 19 — *Baron Komura to Mr. Kurino.*

Tokyo, October 16, 1903.

(Telegram.)

In reference to my telegram of the 8th instant, negotiations are now going on between Baron Rosen and myself regarding the following proposals, which I had presented as amendment to the Russian Counter-Proposals : —

Article II. Insert the phrase " including military assistance" between " assistance" and " to Korea." Change the word " civil " into " internal."

Article III. Insert the phrase " the development of" between " impede" and " the commercial." " Undertakings" to be changed into " activities," and " taken " into " to be taken " and " them " into " those interests."

Article IV. Recognition of the right of Japan to send troops to Korea for the purpose mentioned in the preceding Article or for the purpose of suppressing insurrection or disorder calculated to create international complications.

Article VI. Mutual engagement to establish a neutral zone on the Korea-Manchuria frontier extending .... kilometres on each side, into which neutral zone neither of the Contracting Parties shall introduce troops without the consent of the other.

Article VII. To be struck out and replaced by the following three Articles : —

VII. Engagement on the part of Russia to respect China's sovereignty and territorial integrity in Manchuria, and not to interfere with Japan's commercial freedom in Manchuria.

APPENDIX

VIII. Recognition by Japan of Russia's special interests in Manchuria and of the right of Russia to take such measures as may be necessary for the protection of those interests so long as such measures do not infringe the stipulations of the preceding Article.

IX. Mutual engagement not to impede the connection of the Korean railway and the East China railway when those railways shall have been eventually extended to the Yalu.

Article VIII of the Russian Counter-Proposals to be numbered Article X.

No. 20 — *Baron Komura to Mr. Kurino.*

Tokyo, October 22, 1903.

(Telegram.)

THE result of discussions between Baron Rosen and myself on our amendments to the Russian Counter-Proposals is as follows : —

Amendments to Articles II and VI accepted *ad referendum*, Article III accepted, and Article IV reserved for further discussion. It is in Article VII of our amendment to Article VII of the Russian Counter-Proposals that no agreement could be reached, each insisting on the impossibility of accepting the other's proposition. The contention of the Russian Minister is : — 1st, that the Russian Article VII is the only compensation to Russia for the concessions to be made by her in respect of Korea; and 2d, that admission of the Japanese amendments on this point would be contrary to the principle always insisted on by Russia that the question concerning Manchuria is one exclusively for Russia and China, admitting of no interference on the part of any third Power.

Our contention is:—1st, that Japan does not ask for any concession from Russia with respect to Manchuria, her proposal being simply to have confirmed in the agreement the principle which has been voluntarily and repeatedly declared by Russia; and 2d, that Japan possesses in Manchuria her treaty rights and commercial interests, and she must obtain from Russia a guarantee for the security of those rights and interests as well as of the independence of Korea which would be constantly menaced by Russia's definitive occupation of Manchuria.

No. 21 — *Baron Komura to Mr. Kurino.*

TOKYO, October 29, 1903.

(Telegram.)

IN reference to my telegram of the 22d instant, as the result of further discussions, the amendment on Article IV was finally accepted *ad referendum*. Regarding Article VI, my proposal of fixing the extent of the neutral zone at fifty kilometres on each side of the frontier was accepted *ad referendum*. As to Article VII, no agreement could yet be reached.

No. 22 — *Baron Komura to Mr. Kurino.*

TOKYO, October 30, 1903.

(Telegram.)

I PRESENTED to Baron Rosen on the 30th instant the following as definite amendments of the Imperial Government to the Russian Counter-Proposals:—

APPENDIX

1. Mutual engagement to respect the independence and territorial integrity of the Chinese and Korean Empires.

2. Recognition by Russia of Japan's preponderating interests in Korea and of the right of Japan to give to Korea advice and assistance, including military assistance, tending to improve the administration of the Korean Empire.

3. Engagement on the part of Russia not to impede the development of the commercial and industrial activities of Japan in Korea, nor to oppose any measures taken for the purpose of protecting those interests.

4. Recognition by Russia of the right of Japan to send troops to Korea for the purpose mentioned in the preceding Article or for the purpose of suppressing insurrection or disorder calculated to create international complications.

5. Engagement on the part of Japan not to undertake on the coasts of Korea any military works capable of menacing the freedom of navigation in the Straits of Korea.

6. Mutual engagement to establish a neutral zone on the Korea-Manchurian frontier extending fifty kilometres on each side, into which neutral zone neither of the Contracting Parties shall introduce troops without the consent of the other.

7. Recognition by Japan that Manchuria is outside her sphere of special interest, and recognition by Russia that Korea is outside her sphere of special interest.

8. Recognition by Japan of Russia's special interests in Manchuria and of the right of Russia to take such

measures as may be necessary for the protection of those interests.

9. Engagement on the part of Japan not to interfere with the commercial and residential rights and immunities belonging to Russia in virtue of her treaty engagements with Korea, and engagement on the part of Russia not to interfere with the commercial and residential rights and immunities belonging to Japan in virtue of her treaty engagements with China.

10. Mutual engagement not to impede the connection of the Korean railway and the East China railway when those railways shall have been eventually extended to the Yalu.

11. This agreement to supplant all previous agreements between Japan and Russia respecting Korea.

No. 23 — *Baron Komura to Mr. Kurino.*

TOKYO, November 1, 1903.

(Telegram.)

BARON ROSEN called on me October 31st and stated that the definite proposals which I presented to him as amendments to the Russian proposals as reported in my telegram of the 30th of October were beyond his instructions, and that he would, November 1st, telegraph the full text of the said proposals to his government and ask for further instructions. Accordingly you are instructed to see as soon as possible the Acting Minister for Foreign Affairs in the absence of Count Lamsdorff, and say to him that in preparing the proposals in question, the Japanese Government did not fail to take into full consideration

APPENDIX

the wishes of the Russian Government. You will inform him that in proposing a joint engagement to respect the independence and territorial integrity of China equally with Korea, the Japanese Government were merely asking a reaffirmation of declarations already spontaneously made by Russia, and when it is considered that Russia is prepared to make such an engagement respecting Korea, the reason for excluding China is not understood. The Japanese Government are prepared to admit that the Manchurian question, so far as it does not affect their rights and interests, is purely a Russo-Chinese question; but Japan has extensive and important rights and interests in that region, and the Japanese Government think that in declaring that Manchuria is outside their sphere of special interest, they are at least entitled to ask for a correlative engagement on the part of Russia not to interfere with the commercial and residential rights and immunities belonging to Japan in virtue of her treaty engagements with China. You will in addition point out that the invitation of the Japanese Government, which originated the present negotiations, had in view a definition of the special interest of Japan and Russia in those regions of the far East where the interests of the two Powers meet. The Japanese Government could not have anticipated that the Russian Government, in accepting that invitation, would wish — as might be inferred from Article VII of their Counter-Proposals — to restrict the proposed definition exclusively to the region in which Japan possesses special interests.

CORRESPONDENCE

No. 24 — *Mr. Kurino to Baron Komura.*

PETERSBURG, November 3, 1903.
Received, November 3, 1903.

(Telegram.)

I SAW the Acting Minister for Foreign Affairs on the 2d of November. He said, as his personal opinion, that Japan is making the same demands only in different form and that those demands are too great. I asked in what respects the Japanese Government are considered to be demanding too much, and I added that we do not ask anything more than the recognition of existing treaty rights and immunities of Japan in Manchuria. He then stated that Baron Rosen had said nothing on the subject. The only difficulty, he said, is the connection of the Korean and Manchurian railways. To my question whether there are no other difficulties, he answered that the railway question is the only difficulty, although it had been accepted *ad referendum;* and in conclusion I asked him to use his best influence for the satisfactory solution of the question, as the Japanese Government are fully animated by the spirit of conciliation, and I urged him to advise Count Lamsdorff in the same sense, and if possible to approach the Emperor of Russia on the question. He said that he is willing to do so, and added that Count Lamsdorff will return at the end of this week.

No. 25 — *Mr. Kurino to Baron Komura.*

PETERSBURG, November 13, 1903.
Received, November 13, 1903.

(Telegram.)

I SAW Count Lamsdorff November 12th, and asked whether he had received a copy of the telegram which I had

[227]

APPENDIX

handed to Prince Obolensky and whether any action had been taken in the matter. He answered that he had submitted the telegram to the Emperor, and that before his departure from Darmstadt, he sent under an Imperial order instructions to Baron Rosen to continue negotiations with the Japanese Government. I asked him whether it is on the basis of our last proposal that Baron Rosen was instructed to go on negotiating. Count Lamsdorff said that Baron Rosen had been ordered by the Emperor to examine our last proposal with Admiral Alexieff and to make modification if necessary, and added that at this moment Baron Rosen and Admiral Alexieff must be engaged in the preparation of Counter-Proposals. I remarked to Count Lamsdorff that according to the view of Prince Obolensky, the connection of Korean and Manchurian railways is the question that divides the two governments; but the Japanese Government having subsequently modified the article relating to the question, I cannot believe that it is the principal point on which an agreement cannot be established. Count Lamsdorff replied that he thinks for his part that it is the Manchurian question which divides the two parties, as he had said from the very beginning the Russian Government consider always that this question is a question exclusively between Russia and China, and it must be reserved to his government to take all proper measures to safeguard their very considerable interests in Manchuria by means of an arrangement with China. I explained to him that Japan is ever ready to recognise the special and considerable interests which Russia has in Manchuria, and that she has no intention whatever of trespassing upon them, but that Japan has a perfect right to demand that the independence and territorial integrity of China shall be respected and the rights and the interests of Japan in that region shall be formally guaranteed. Count Lamsdorff answered that the objection relates to the form rather than the substance of the proposal. In Manchuria other Powers also have rights and interests, and Russia cannot enter into special arrangement with each of those Powers regarding Manchuria. I observed that should the Russian Government be in accord with Japan in principle, it is deeply to be regretted that an understanding cannot be reached, merely because of failure to find a suitable formula by which to bring the two governments to an arrangement, and that I could not but ardently ask him to use his influence to bring about a satisfactory solution according to the principles already admitted by Russia.

No. 26 — *Baron Komura to Mr. Kurino.*

TOKYO, November 21, 1903.

(Telegram.)

BARON ROSEN informed me on November 20th, that he received a telegram November 14th, from Admiral Alexieff to the effect that Admiral Alexieff had already forwarded the Counter-Proposals to St. Petersburg. Baron Rosen added that he had not yet received any instructions on the subject of the Counter-Proposals. Consequently you are instructed to see Count Lamsdorff as soon as possible, and after explaining to him Baron Rosen's statements as above, you will say that the Japanese Government are anxious to proceed with the negotiations with all possible expedition; and you will urge him to exert his influence to secure the early despatch of instructions to Baron Rosen in order that the negotiations may be resumed and concluded without delay.

No. 27 — *Mr. Kurino to Baron Komura.*

PETERSBURG, November 22, 1903.
Received, November 23, 1903.

(Telegram.)

I SAW Count Lamsdorff on the 22d of November. He said that the modifications are already in the hands of the Emperor; but on account of the illness of the Empress, the former does not attend to any business affairs; hence the delay. I asked him to use his best endeavours to obtain the earliest possible Imperial order on the question. He said in reply that it will be better for me to write him a note giving the purport of instructions I have received from you; then he will immediately send it to the Emperor. At the end of the conversation I asked whether it is not possible for me to get some information about the modifications proposed by Admiral Alexieff. He seemed rather puzzled to give a direct answer; but he said that the Russian Government are ready to enter into immediate agreement with Japan regarding Korea, even making large concessions, but as to Manchuria, Russia once took possession of the country by right of conquest; nevertheless, she is willing to restore it to China, but with certain guarantees assuring security to the enormous interests which Russia has in Manchuria. While China is still insisting upon her refusal to give such guarantees, it is not possible for Russia to come to any arrangement with a third Power respecting Manchuria, as the question is exclusively between the two countries concerned. Then I said that if I accurately judge the nature of our proposition, it is not the intention of the Japanese Government to interfere with direct negotiations between the two governments concerned, as may be seen from the first part of Article VII of our last proposition; but we only wish the independence and integrity of China, as repeatedly declared on the part of Russia, and security for our important interests in that province. This is not for the purpose of interfering with the affairs of the two Powers concerned, but only to prevent misunderstanding between Russia and Japan regarding the province where both Powers have some interest; and I added that if in principle such an *entente* could in some form or other be arrived at perhaps even negotiations between Russia and China might be more easily carried out. He thereupon repeated his request for me to write him a note as above mentioned, and that I should add my own opinion in it, and that he would immediately send it to the Emperor. He told me that he expects to have audience on the 25th of November at Skernevice and that the note could be sent to him towards this evening. I judge from the tone of Count Lamsdorff's conversation that the modifications proposed by Admiral Alexieff will not be favourable to our proposition regarding China and Manchuria.

APPENDIX

No. 28 — *Baron Komura to Mr. Kurino.*

TOKYO, November 28, 1903.

(Telegram.)

You report in your telegram of November 22d that Count Lamsdorff expected to have audience of the Emperor on the 25th instant. Accordingly you are instructed to see Count Lamsdorff as soon as possible and ask him what action has been taken regarding further instructions to Baron Rosen.

No. 29 — *Mr. Kurino to Baron Komura.*

PETERSBURG, November 27, 1903.
Received, November 28, 1903.

Telegram.)

COUNT Lamsdorff told me he did not see the Emperor November 25th, on account of the sickness of the Empress. Interior inflammation of her right ear has necessitated an operation. He said that he immediately despatched to the Emperor my note mentioned in my telegram of November 22d.

No. 30 — *Baron Komura to Mr. Kurino.*

TOKYO, December 1, 1903.

(Telegram.)

THE Japanese Government have from the first attached the highest importance to a speedy solution of the questions which form at this time the subject of negotiations between Japan and Russia. It seemed to them that in a matter of such vital moment as that which engages the attention of the Cabinets of Tokyo and St. Petersburg, a quick conclusion was only second in importance to a satisfactory conclusion. Consistently with that view the Japanese Government have at all times during the progress of the negotiations made it a special point to give prompt answers to all propositions of the Russian Government. The negotiations have now been pending for no less than four months, and they have not yet reached a stage where the final issue can with certainty be predicted. In these circumstances the Japanese Government cannot but regard with grave concern the situation for which the delays in negotiations are largely responsible. You are instructed to see Count Lamsdorff as soon as possible and place the foregoing considerations before him in such form and manner as to make your representations as impressive as possible. You will add that the Japanese Government believe they are rendering service to the general interest in thus frankly explaining to the Russian Government the actual state of things.

No. 31 — *Mr. Kurino to Baron Komura.*

PETERSBURG, December 2, 1903.
Received, December 3, 1903.

(Telegram.)

I HEARD that the Russian Government are still repeatedly communicating with Admiral Alexieff.

No. 32 — *Mr. Kurino to Baron Komura.*

PETERSBURG, December 4, 1903.
Received, December 4, 1903.

(Telegram.)

COUNT LAMSDORFF received me on the night of December 3d. I handed him a French translation of your telegram of December 1st together with a letter which I addressed to

[233]

him expressing fully the pressing situation under which the Japanese Government are now labouring. He said that the question requires consideration still, and he is in communication with Admiral Alexieff; but the Emperor is to return December 5th, and he said that he will fully explain the urgency of the matter on the occasion of his audience on the following Tuesday. He thinks he will then be able to send instructions to Baron Rosen. To my question whether it is not possible for him to have audience at an earlier date, he said that Saturday is the fête of the Crown Prince, no business is transacted on Sunday, and he will be occupied with other affairs on Monday. He promised to let me know the result of his audience next Wednesday.

No. 33 — *Mr. Kurino to Baron Komura.*

PETERSBURG, December 9, 1903.
Received, December 10, 1903.

(Telegram.)

COUNT LAMSDORFF told me December 9th that an Imperial order had been sent yesterday to Admiral Alexieff and Baron Rosen to continue the negotiations in accordance with the Counter-Proposals of Admiral Alexieff, but that the Japanese propositions have been fully considered. I asked whether he could inform me of the nature of the propositions on which Baron Rosen is authorized to continue the negotiations. He said that they will be officially communicated within two or three days through Baron Rosen to the Japanese Government.

CORRESPONDENCE

No. 84 — *Baron Komura to Mr. Kurino.*

Tokyo, December 12, 1903.

(Telegram.)

Baron Rosen called on me December 11th and, under instructions of his government, officially presented to me the following Counter-Proposals of the Russian Government in reply to our definitive amendments as stated in my telegram of October 30th : —

1. Mutual engagement to respect the independence and territorial integrity of the Korean Empire.

2. Recognition by Russia of Japan's preponderating interests in Korea and of the right of Japan to assist Korea with advice tending to improve the civil administration.

3. Engagement on the part of Russia not to oppose the development of the industrial and commercial activities of Japan in Korea, nor the adoption of measures for the protection of those interests.

4. Recognition by Russia of the right of Japan to send troops to Korea for the purpose mentioned in the preceding article, or for the purpose of suppressing insurrections or disorders capable of creating international complications.

5. Mutual engagement not to make use of any part of the Korean territory for strategical purposes, and not to undertake on the Korean coast any military works capable of menacing the freedom of navigation in the Straits of Korea.

6. Mutual engagement to consider the territory of Korea to the north of the 39th parallel as a neutral zone, within the limits of which neither of the contracting parties shall introduce troops.

[235]

APPENDIX

7. Mutual engagement not to impede the connection of the Korean and East China Railways, when those railways shall have been extended to the Yalu.

8. Abrogation of all previous agreements between Russia and Japan respecting Korea.

No. 85 — *Baron Komura to Mr. Kurino.*

Tokyo, December 21, 1903.

(Telegram.)

In an interview with the Russian Minister, December 21st, I pointed out the fundamental difference in territorial compass between Japan's original proposals and Russia's new Counter-Proposals, and after fully explaining the reasons which induced the Japanese Government to believe it to be desirable in the general interest to include in the proposed understanding all regions in the extreme East where the interests of the two empires meet, I expressed the hope that the Russian Government would reconsider their position regarding that branch of the question. I also informed him fully respecting the amendments which the Japanese Government consider it necessary to introduce into Russia's new Counter-Proposals. Accordingly, in order to remove every possibility of misunderstanding on the part of Russia respecting the attitude of the Japanese Government, you are instructed to deliver to Count Lamsdorff a Note Verbale to the following effect : —

"The Imperial Government have examined with great care and attention the new Russian Counter-Proposals of the 11th instant. They regret to find that the Imperial Russian Government did not see their way in those pro-

[236]

posals to give to the compass of the suggested understanding the same territorial extension as was deemed essential by Japan. The Imperial Government, in their original invitation to the Imperial Russian Government in August last, endeavoured to make it entirely clear that they desired, with a view to remove from their relations with the Imperial Russian Government every cause for future misunderstanding, to bring within the purview of the proposed arrangement all those regions in the extreme East where the interests of the two empires meet, and they cannot bring themselves to the conviction that a full realisation of that desire can be expected if a large and important portion of those regions is wholly excluded from consideration. Accordingly, the Imperial Government feel constrained to ask the Imperial Russian Government to reconsider their position on the subject, and they hope that the Russian Government will be able to see their way to arrive at a satisfactory solution of the question. The Imperial Government also find it necessary to ask for the following amendments to the new Russian Counter-Proposals : —

"*a.* ARTICLE II to read : 'Recognition by Russia of Japan's preponderating interests in Korea and of the right of Japan to give Korea advice and assistance tending to improve the administration of the Korean Empire.'

"*b.* ARTICLE V to read : 'Mutual engagement not to undertake on the Korean coast any military works capable of menacing the freedom of navigation in the Straits of Korea ;' and

"*c.* ARTICLE VI to be suppressed.

APPENDIX

"As the principal part of these amendments cannot be said to be in excess of the modifications which were agreed to *ad referendum* at Tokyo, and as the Imperial Government consider those changes indispensable, it is hoped that they will receive the ready agreement of the Imperial Russian Government."

In presenting the foregoing note to Count Lamsdorff, you will say that I have spoken to Baron Rosen in a similar sense, and you will also express the desire for an early response.

No. 36 — *Mr. Kurino to Baron Komura.*

PETERSBURG, December 23, 1903.
Received, December 24, 1903.

(Telegram.)

UPON receipt of your telegraphic instructions, I saw Count Lamsdorff December 23d at 2 P. M. He told me he had received a telegram from Baron Rosen, stating that the latter had had an interview with you, and that particulars would follow, but such particulars had not been received yet by him. When I handed him the Note Verbale, he said that he would study it together with report from Baron Rosen, and that he would do his best to send the Russian answer at the earliest possible date; but he added that he would have to communicate with Admiral Alexieff. In conclusion, I stated to him that under the present circumstances it might cause serious difficulties, even complications, if we failed to come to an *entente*, and I hoped he would exercise his best influence so as to enable us to reach the desired end.

CORRESPONDENCE

No. 87 — *Mr. Kurino to Baron Komura.*

PETERSBURG, January 1, 1904.
Received, January 2, 1904.

(Telegram.)

I SAW Count Lamsdorff, January 1st, and asked whether any action had been taken regarding our last propositions. He said they had been fully considered; and he asked me to assure you that Baron Rosen will soon be instructed to proceed with the negotiations in a friendly and conciliatory spirit, and he added that he saw no reason why we could not arrive at an *entente*.

No. 88 — *Baron Komura to Mr. Kurino.*

TOKYO, January 7, 1904.

(Telegram.)

BARON ROSEN handed to me January 6th the following reply of the Russian Government to our last propositions of December 21st last : —

"Having no objection to the amendments to Article II of the Russian Counter-Proposals as proposed by the Imperial Japanese Government, the Imperial Government considers it necessary:

"1. To maintain the original wording of Article V which had already been agreed to by the Imperial Japanese Government, that is to say, 'mutual engagement not to use any part of the territory of Korea for strategical purposes, nor to undertake on the coasts of Korea any military works capable of menacing the freedom of navigation in the Straits of Korea.'

"2. To maintain Article VI concerning a neutral zone (this for the very purpose which the Imperial Japanese Government has likewise in view, that is to say, to eliminate everything that might lead to misunderstandings in the future; a similar

[239]

zone, for example, exists between the Russian and British possessions in central Asia).

" In case the above conditions are agreed to, the Imperial Government would be prepared to include in the projected agreement an Article of the following tenor :

"Recognition by Japan of Manchuria and her littoral as being outside her sphere of interests, whilst Russia, within the limits of that province, will not impede Japan, nor other Powers in the enjoyment of rights and privileges acquired by them under existing treaties with China, exclusive of the establishment of settlements."

No. 39 — *Baron Komura to Mr. Kurino.*

(Telegram.)   TOKYO, January 13, 1904.

You are instructed to deliver to Count Lamsdorff a Note Verbale to the following effect which, you will say, is intended to confirm to him the views of the Imperial Government communicated by me to Baron Rosen on the 13th of January : —

The Imperial Government, in order to arrive at a pacific solution of the pending questions, and to firmly establish the basis of good relation between Japan and Russia, and in addition with a view to protect the rights and interests of Japan, have given most careful and serious consideration to the reply of the Imperial Russian Government which was delivered by His Excellency Baron Rosen on the 6th instant. They have finally come to the conclusion that the following modifications are necessary, *i. e.:* —

1. Suppression of the first clause of Article V of the Russian Counter-Proposals (presented to the Japanese

CORRESPONDENCE

Government through Baron Rosen December 11th), that is to say, "not to use any part of Korean territory for strategical purposes."

2. Suppression of the whole Article (VI) concerning establishment of a neutral zone.

3. The Russian proposal concerning Manchuria to be agreed to with the following modifications:

a. Recognition by Japan of Manchuria and its littoral as being outside her sphere of interest and an engagement on the part of Russia to respect the territorial integrity of China in Manchuria.

b. Russia within the limits of Manchuria will not impede Japan nor other Powers in the enjoyment of rights and privileges acquired by them under the existing treaties with China.

c. Recognition by Russia of Korea and its littoral as being outside her sphere of interest.

4. Addition of an Article to the following effect:

Recognition by Japan of Russia's special interests in Manchuria and of the right of Russia to take measures necessary for the protection of those interests.

The grounds for these amendments having been frequently and fully explained on previous occasions, the Imperial Government do not think it necessary to repeat the explanations. It is sufficient here to express their earnest hope for reconsideration by the Imperial Russian Government.

It should be further remarked that the suppression of the clause excluding the establishment of settlements in Manchuria is desired because it conflicts with stipulations of the new Commercial Treaty between Japan and China. In this respect, however, Japan will be satisfied if she receives equal treatment with another Power which has already acquired similar rights in regard to settlements in Manchuria. The statement in the Russian reply that the Japanese Government have agreed to the original wording of Article V of the Russian Counter-Proposals is erroneous, no such agreement ever having been expressed by the Imperial Government.

The above-mentioned amendments being proposed by the Imperial Government entirely in a spirit of conciliation, it is expected that they will be received with the same spirit at the hands of the Imperial Russian Government; and the Imperial Government further hope for an early reply from the Imperial Russian Government, since further delay in the solution of the question will be extremely disadvantageous to the two countries.

No. 40 — *Baron Komura to Mr. Kurino.*

TOKYO, January 23, 1904.
(Telegram.)
You are instructed to sound Count Lamsdorff respecting the probable nature of Russia's reply to our last note and when the reply will be delivered.

No. 41 — *Mr. Kurino to Baron Komura.*

PETERSBURG, January 25, 1904.
Received, January 25, 1904.
(Telegram.)
In reference to your telegram of 23d instant, I saw Count Lamsdorff January 24th and asked his views in regard to

our last proposals and also how soon the Russian answer could be given. He was not inclined to enter into details, but said that there are certain points to which he could not agree. He expects to lay his views before the Emperor next Tuesday, January 26th, and he hopes to be able to send an answer before long.

M. de Hartwig, whom I saw this afternoon, told me that the Department of Foreign Affairs is yet in communication with Admiral Alexieff, and he cannot say how soon an answer can be sent to Japan.

No. 42 — *Baron Komura to Mr. Kurino.*

TOKYO, January 26, 1904.

(Telegram.)

As the situation admits of no indefinite delay in the settlement of the questions involved, you will seek an interview with Count Lamsdorff at the earliest opportunity and state to him as an instruction from your government that in the opinion of the Imperial Government a further prolongation of the present state of things being calculated to accentuate the gravity of the situation, it is their earnest hope that they will be honoured with an early reply, and that they wish to know at what time they may expect to receive the reply.

No. 43 — *Mr. Kurino to Baron Komura.*

PETERSBURG, January 26, 1904.
Received, January 27, 1904.

(Telegram.)

IN reference to your telegram of the 26th instant, the Russian Minister for Foreign Affairs said that the Ministers of War, Marine and other authorities concerned are to meet on the 28th of January for the consideration of the question, and that their decision will be submitted to the Emperor for sanction, and he remarked that it had been the intention of Admiral Alexieff to come here; but that that idea was now abandoned, and his opinion will soon be received by telegraph. Under these circumstances, he says, he is unable to give the exact date when the reply will be given; but he can say it will not be much delayed. He said that he had received reports from official sources to the effect that Japan had sent a considerable number of troops, munitions and war materials to Korea, and asked me whether I could give any explanation regarding it. I simply answered that I knew nothing of such facts, and regretted not being able to give him any explanation. He added that such action on the part of Japan causes a very bad impression, while the two governments are engaged seriously in such important negotiations. Telegraph me for my information whether the reports are true, and if so, the details.

No. 44 — *Baron Komura to Mr. Kurino.*

TOKYO, January 28, 1904.

(Telegram.)

IN reference to your telegram of 26th instant, you will see Count Lamsdorff at an early opportunity and say to him that you have been authorized to deny positively the statement that Japan has sent to Korea a considerable number of troops, munitions and war materials. As a matter of fact, no troops have recently been sent to Korea nor any ammunitions have been sent beyond the amount required for the ordinary use of the Japanese troops stationed in Korea. You will then ask him whether the report that Russian troops are being concentrated on the Korean frontier is true, and if so, that such military movement is to be highly deprecated. Finally, you will ask him whether he is not able to acquaint you, for your own information, with the nature of the decision taken at the proposed conference of the ministers on the 28th of January, and whether he can indicate the approximate date on which the Russian reply is to be given.

No. 45 — *Mr. Kurino to Baron Komura.*

PETERSBURG, January 28, 1904.
Received, January 29, 1904.

(Telegram.)

COUNT LAMSDORFF is satisfied with the explanation contained in your telegram of to-day. As to the question regarding the concentration of Russian troops near the Yalu, he does not believe it to be true, and he remarked that such newspaper reports are very regrettable. I tried to obtain information about the decision of to-day's meeting. He said that it is not possible for him to say anything concerning it as it will not be sent to the Emperor, and that until the respective ministers have been received by the Emperor respecting the question, nothing can be said definitely. He stated that the Grand Duke Alexis and the Minister of Marine are to be received in audience next Monday, and the Minister of War and himself on Tuesday; and he thinks an answer will be sent to Admiral Alexieff on the latter day. I pointed out the urgent necessity to accelerate the despatch of an answer as much as possible, because further prolongation of the present condition is not only undesirable but rather dangerous. I added that all the while the world is loud with rumours and that I hoped he would take special steps so as to have an answer sent at an earlier date than mentioned. He replied that he knows the existing condition of things very well, but that the dates of audience being fixed as above mentioned, it is not now possible to change them; and he repeated that he will do his best to send the reply next Tuesday.

No. 46 — *Baron Komura to Mr. Kurino.*

TOKYO, January 30, 1904.

(Telegram.)

IN reference to your telegram of January 28th, you are instructed to see Count Lamsdorff at the earliest opportunity and state to him substantially in the following sense : —

" Having reported to your government that the Russian Government would probably give a reply on next Tuesday you have been instructed to say to Count Lamsdorff that being fully convinced of the serious disadvantage to the two Powers concerned of the further prolongation of the present situation, the Imperial Government hoped that they might be able to receive the reply of the Russian Government earlier than the date mentioned by Count Lamsdorff. As it, however, appears that the receipt of the reply at an earlier date is not possible, the Imperial Government wish to know whether they will be honoured with the reply at the date mentioned by Count Lamsdorff, namely, next Tuesday, or if it is not possible, what will be the exact date on which the reply is to be given."

If Count Lamsdorff specifies the day on which the reply is to be given, you will see him on that day and ask him to acquaint you with the exact nature of the reply.

No. 47 — *Mr. Kurino to Baron Komura.*

PETERSBURG, February 1, 1904.
Received, February 1, 1904.

(Telegram.)

REGARDING your telegram of the 30th of January, I saw Count Lamsdorff in the evening of January 31st. He says he appreciates fully the gravity of the present situation, and is certainly desirous to send an answer as quickly as possible; but the question is a very serious one and is not to be lightly dealt with. In addition, the opinions of the ministers concerned and Admiral Alexieff had to be brought into harmony; hence the natural delay. As to the date of sending an answer, he says, it is not possible for him to give the exact date as it entirely depends upon the decision of the Emperor, though he will not fail to use his efforts to hurry the matter.

No. 48 — *Baron Komura to Mr. Kurino.*

TOKYO, February 5, 1904.   2.15 P. M.

(Telegram.)

FURTHER prolongation of the present situation being inadmissible, the Imperial Government have decided to terminate the pending negotiations and to take such independent action as they may deem necessary to defend

APPENDIX

their menaced position and to protect their rights and interests. Accordingly you are instructed to address to Count Lamsdorff, immediately upon receipt of this telegram, a signed note to the following effect: —

"The undersigned, Envoy Extraordinary and Minister Plenipotentiary of His Majesty the Emperor of Japan, has the honour, in pursuance of instructions from his government, to address to His Excellency the Minister for Foreign Affairs of His Majesty the Emperor of all the Russias the following communications: —

"The government of His Majesty the Emperor of Japan regard the independence and territorial integrity of the Empire of Korea as essential to their own repose and safety, and they are consequently unable to view with indifference any action tending to render the position of Korea insecure.

"The successive rejections by the Imperial Russian Government by means of inadmissible amendments of Japan's proposals respecting Korea, the adoption of which the Imperial Government regarded as indispensable to assure the independence and territorial integrity of the Korean Empire and to safeguard Japan's preponderating interests in the peninsula, coupled with the successive refusals of the Imperial Russian Government to enter into engagements to respect China's territorial integrity in Manchuria, which is seriously menaced by their continued occupation of the province, notwithstanding their treaty engagements with China and their repeated assurances to other Powers possessing interests in those regions, have made it necessary for the Imperial Government seriously to consider what measures of self-defence they are called upon to take.

"In the presence of delays which remain largely unexplained and naval and military activities which it is difficult to reconcile with entirely pacific aims, the Imperial Government have exercised in the depending negotiations a degree of forbearance which they believe affords abundant proof of their loyal desire to remove from their relations with the Imperial Russian Government every cause for future misunderstanding. But finding in their efforts no prospect of securing from the Imperial Russian Government an adhesion either to Japan's moderate and unselfish proposals or to any other proposals likely to establish a firm and enduring peace in the extreme East, the Imperial Government have no other alternative than to terminate the present futile negotiations.

"In adopting that course the Imperial Government reserve to themselves the right to take such independent action as they may deem best to consolidate and defend their menaced position, as well as to protect their established rights and legitimate interests.

"The undersigned, etc., etc."

No. 49 — *Baron Komura to Mr. Kurino.*

TOKYO, February 5, 1904.   2.15 P. M.

(Telegram.)

You are instructed to address to Count Lamsdorff a signed note to the following effect simultaneously with the note mentioned in my previous telegram : —

APPENDIX

"The undersigned, Envoy Extraordinary and Minister Plenipotentiary of His Majesty the Emperor of Japan, has the honour, in pursuance of instructions from his government, to acquaint His Excellency the Minister for Foreign Affairs of His Majesty the Emperor of all the Russias that the Imperial Government of Japan, having exhausted without effect every means of conciliation with a view to the removal from their relations with the Imperial Russian Government of every cause for future complications, and finding that their just representations and moderate and unselfish proposals in the interest of a firm and lasting peace in the extreme East are not receiving the consideration which is their due, have resolved to sever their diplomatic relations with the Imperial Russian Government which for the reason named have ceased to possess any value.

"In further fulfilment of the command of his government, the undersigned has also the honour to announce to His Excellency Count Lamsdorff that it is his intention to take his departure from St. Petersburg with the staff of the Imperial Legation on . . . date.

"The undersigned, etc., etc."

No. 50 — *Mr. Kurino to Baron Komura.*

PETERSBURG, February 5, 1904.   5.05 A. M.
Received, February 5, 1904.   5.15 P. M.

(Telegram.)

IN compliance with the request of Count Lamsdorff, I went to see him at 8 P. M. February 4th. He told me that the substance of the Russian answer had been just sent to

CORRESPONDENCE

Admiral Alexieff to be transmitted to Baron Rosen. He added that Admiral Alexieff may happen to introduce some changes so as to meet local circumstances; but in all probability there will be no such changes. He then stated as his own opinion that Russia desires the principle of independence and integrity of Korea and also, of necessity, the free passage of the Korean Straits. Though Russia is willing to make every possible concession, she does not desire to see Korea utilised for strategic purposes against Russia, and believes it useful for the consolidation of good relations with Japan to establish by common accord a buffer region between confines of direct influence and action of the two countries in the far East. The above is expressed entirely as his personal opinion, and I cannot say whether the same is the substance of the above-mentioned answer, though it seems to be very probable.

No. 51 — *Mr. Kurino to Baron Komura.*

PETERSBURG, February 6, 1904. 5.57 P. M.
Received, February 7, 1904. 5.45 A. M.

(Telegram.)

IN reference to your two telegrams of yesterday's date, I presented to Count Lamsdorff to-day at 4 P. M. the notes as instructed. I shall withdraw from here with my staff and students on the 10th instant.

Lightning Source UK Ltd.
Milton Keynes UK
UKOW021944111212

203533UK00008B/632/P